Memoirs of a Century

Memoirs of a Century

Sir Jack Harris Bt

STEELE ROBERTS
AOTEAROA NEW ZEALAND

*This story is dedicated to
my children: Christopher, Margaret, and Paul;
my grandsons: Andrew, Mark, Matthew, Nick and Sam;
my granddaughters: Charlotte, Phoebe and Sophie;
my great-grandchildren: Arthur, George, Hannah, Madeleine
and Sophie; and to future generations*

© Sir Jack Harris 2007

Cover: Sir Jack Harris and Te Rama.
Thanks to Peter Acland, Matthew Bartlett, Colin Bassett, Torsten Fischer, Alex Harris, Margaret Harris, Paul Harris, Faith Lawton, and Beverley and Hugh Price for production assistance.

National Library of New Zealand Cataloguing-in-Publication Data
Harris, Jack, Sir, 1906-
Memoirs of a century / Sir Jack Harris.
Includes index.
ISBN 978-1-877448-04-1
1. Harris, Jack, Sir, 1906- 2. New Zealand—economic conditions —
20th century. 3. New Zealand—Politics and government—20th century.
4. New Zealand—History—20th century. I. Title.
993.03—dc 22

STEELE ROBERTS LTD
Box 9321, Wellington, Aotearoa New Zealand
info@steeleroberts.co.nz • www.steeleroberts.co.nz
in association with Gondwanaland Press

CONTENTS

I	Grandparents	7
II	Parents	13
III	My early life	25
IV	Bing Harris 1858–1929	37
V	Starting life in New Zealand	46
VI	Depression, the first Labour government, and war	59
VII	People, politics, and events in Europe between the wars	67
VIII	Bing Harris — after the war to 1979	77
IX	Scenes from the East	87
X	Sketches of politics and social life 1940s–1980s	92
XI	Te Rama, Waikanae	102
XII	Patricia's story of Te Rama	110
XIII	Doomsday	130
	APPENDIX: *Lady Harris's obituary*	137
	INDEX	140

Sir Jack Harris Bt, 2007.

I
Grandparents

Wolf Harris, my grandfather on my father's side, was somewhat of a mystery because my Victorian-born father did not think his origins were reputable.

Grandfather was born in Cracow, then a part of Austria, now part of Poland. His family were respectable Jews. His father, I believe, was a rabbi, and Grandfather was certainly not uneducated. He spoke English well and his letters were very literate. His ability to earn a fortune enabled my father to go to school at Harrow and then on to Cambridge. Grandfather's main interest outside business was collecting paintings, and he was an Associate of the Royal Academy. His pictures went out of fashion, but some in the collection have since become recognised as significant works and hang in the Dunedin Art Gallery.

As far as I can find out, Wolf Harris left Cracow in 1848, a year of revolution. I expect that life was a bit hot in Poland with the Russians, Germans and Austrians squabbling over which pieces of the prostrate country were theirs. He arrived in Australia in 1848 and I suspect he jumped ship. He is first heard of in Bendigo, probably making a precarious living hawking imported goods to the miners. Later he came to New Zealand when gold was found here; again I am not sure when. One report gives 1852 and another

1858. The Pioneer Club records give 1858, so maybe that is right. On the other hand he was apparently negotiating a partnership with a P Hayman as early as 1856. He used to travel all over the country selling goods and was friendly with the Maori people. I can remember as a boy going with my grandfather to the Wembley exhibition where there was a Maori exhibit, and he spoke to the Maori people there in their language.

When he had a little money, he bought an interest in the firm of Turnbull Bing in Wellington and soon bought out Turnbull. Bing Harris was founded in 1858, and continued, for a large part of the time under my control, until it was bought out by Brierleys in 1977.

In 1871, Grandfather married Elizabeth Nathan, the daughter of David Nathan, founder of L D Nathan in Auckland, one of the first firms in New Zealand, dating back to the 1830s. In the 1870s, there was a British army garrison in Auckland and apparently Granny liked the garrison very much and her parents decided she had to be married off quickly. And they looked around, saw my grandfather, and that was that. It was all arranged and it worked out all right. This was the first Jewish marriage celebrated in New Zealand.

Soon after the formation of the firm, Grandfather appointed a partner and went to do the buying in London. The firm went through bad times during this period, but somehow survived. It certainly managed to make some profits, but was quite small, as was the population of New Zealand.

Grandfather did make enough money, however, to buy a huge house in Queensgate in London. It had a ballroom, dining room and sitting rooms. My father remembered that his parents were very social and used to hold large balls. I don't think either Grandfather or Granny were much interested in religion, although Grandfather became more interested as he grew older but he never interfered with his children's religious activities or their lack of them. He was a very generous man, supporting numerous charities, as well as providing handsomely for his family.

Our routine was that my brother Nicholas and I would have dinner with my grandparents on Sundays, which I liked because of the rich food. I was very greedy and their chocolate pudding was a highlight. The house was full of huge vases and I was always knocking them over, occasionally smashing one.

They had two ancient retainers: Hannah the cook and Geisler the butler. Poor Geisler was interned during World War I because he was German. Grandfather managed to escape internment.

I remember the 'Old Man' quite well. I used to play bridge with him and his wife in the boudoir. He died in 1926 when he was 93, which seemed an enormous age, and now I am already much older than that! He took a great personal interest in Dunedin: he gave his home and freehold property to the first Karitane Hospital, he presented pictures to the Dunedin Art Gallery, endowed the chair of physiology at Otago University, and presented a fountain which is in the Botanical Gardens. I need not add that it was his initiative which created the business which prospered under his control until age caught up with him.

My mother's father, Grandfather Bloxham, had a very different background. The Bloxham family came from the Cotswolds, where they had lived almost since William the Conqueror's time. Traditionally, they were in the legal profession and were associated with the wool trade. They had large long-living families. Great-grandfather moved to Marlow in the Chilterns and set up as a solicitor there. I can just remember his home, a lovely 18th-century house. As a boy, Grandfather went to school in Maidenhead and later went to Highgate School, a tradition of the Bloxhams. He went to school in a coach and then to Maidenhead by train. I remember him telling me that in the back of the coach was a man armed with a blunderbuss to protect them from highwaymen as they passed through Maidenhead Thicket.

Grandfather studied medicine and paid for his medical studies by playing billiards for money around the pubs. He was thrown out of his home for dissecting a body on the diningroom table. He was surgeon to the Blues Regiment for about two years. It must have been during this period he began to study syphilis, an unmentionable subject in Victorian England. He published three papers on the subject and was the first person in England to use skin grafts. An acquaintance of mine told me of the time Grandfather operated on him. He was told in a stentorian voice to take his pants down, and in a lightning move a piece of skin was removed from his bottom and transferred to the affected place. The operation was a success.

Grandfather retired early and bought an Elizabethan house in Bourne End, near Hemel Hempstead, which had once been an inn. There was a cockfighting room and Grandfather added a billiard room decorated with huge pike he had caught. The house had a beautiful garden where he exercised his surgical skills in grafting plants. He had distinguished friends in the country where he would go hunting and fishing.

He was a convinced atheist and would shout people down with "God damn rot, bloody nonsense!" Granny Bloxham, on the other hand, was very religious; her name was Jessica Porter and she brought with her a very welcome dowry — surgeons were not well paid in Victorian England. Her family owned Foster Porter, and Mr Porter was a close friend of Grandfather. I believe it was because of that association that Father met and married my mother Frieda.

GRANDPARENTS

Wolf Harris.

Sir Percy Harris Bt.

II

Parents

My father, the Rt Hon Percy A Harris MP

My father was born in Queensgate, London in about 1877, and educated at Harrow and Trinity Hall, Cambridge. Trinity Hall was at that time focused on rowing. Education was of little importance to the college, provided you rowed. My father, as might be expected from one brought up in London in a home not dedicated to sport, did not participate in sport and therefore was ridiculed by his fellow undergraduates. He was moved to digs above the senior tutor rooms to enable him to continue his studies for a law degree.

Despite the contempt of the rowing fraternity, Trinity Hall continued to be the leading law college at the university. A degree obtained by a Trinity student made it likely that the student would become a judge. The university's hold on the legal profession was very strong and was one of the ways the establishment retained its control.

My father had other ideas about his studies for law; he wished to enter politics as a radical liberal with very left-wing views, which were at odds with much of the opinion of that time. He would spend his vacations working as a volunteer at the charitable institution TOC House in the East End of London, and it was there that he started his lifelong association with Bethnal Green.

However, my grandfather persuaded my father to start work at Bing Harris's London office. My grandfather ran the London office and did not want to return to New Zealand, and it was logical that his sons should settle in New Zealand and run the business there.

After my father married my mother, Frieda Bloxham, my grandfather sent him to New Zealand, to the Dunedin office of the firm. My father had been brought up in London and the culture shock on arriving in New Zealand must have been tremendous. It was a very remote place. The only contact with the rest of the world was by mail, as I found out later myself.

The Presbyterian Church dominated Dunedin. All mention of sex was frowned upon — even at the beach standards of modesty were enforced. Everyone entertained everyone and as my father did not drink or play sport, and was not in the least interested in the business except as a source of income, life was depressing and lonely for him. My mother was equally unable to adjust to New Zealand.

Given these circumstances my grandfather was persuaded to let my father return to England and he was given a nominal job in the London office, from which he drew his income. Percy was fortunate that his father was so understanding, thus enabling him to pursue a political career — MPs at the time earned no salary — and the Liberal Party gave him the opportunity to stand for the electorate of Ashford as candidate.

I was born in 1906 just before the election and my mother would bring Baby Harris to all election meetings. I was named Ashford after the electorate. Unfortunately this was not sufficient to enable my father to be elected to parliament! He did succeed in being elected to the London County Council, of which he remained a member for about 50 years. At one time he became deputy leader of the council when the Liberals were in power.

My earliest memory — I was three — is being there when Edward VII laid the foundation stone for the new London County Council building. I vaguely remember a fat old gentleman with a beard. He was, in fact, Emperor of India and ruler of a huge empire on which the sun never set, and thus one of the most important people in the world, though apparently he was not in the least arrogant. He was a bit of a playboy, enjoying women and wine, and was much liked as he had an easy manner with people.

The London County Council governed London, which excluded the City, with extreme efficiency and London had a reputation as one of the best-governed cities in the world. There was little crime and the city was clean and tidy. It had a good water supply, a good education system and good amenities. This continued until the arrival of Mrs Thatcher, when London County committed the 'sin' of electing a Labour council. She abolished the council in 1986.

At one time my father had the distinction of being the one Liberal on the council who held the balance of power between the Conservative and the Labour parties. Because the party in office, which at that time was the Conservatives, had the power to appoint aldermen (which was hardly democratic), they retained control of the council.

My father wished to pursue his political career by standing for parliament for Bethnal Green, which he already represented on the London County Council, but party HQ thought otherwise. They sent down a man called Masterman, who was unknown to the electorate, to stand for the seat. He promptly lost it to the Conservatives.

As compensation my father was given the seat of Market Harborough by the party, where he was likewise totally unknown. He managed to win this seat because there was a big Liberal swing when the Asquith government was elected in 1908. However, in a swing back in the next election he lost his seat. Fortunately for him the seat of South West Bethnal Green became vacant.

Percy had retained his connection with the electorate through his membership of London County Council and was already well known there. This time he won the election and held the seat until 1945, just after World War II. Some years after he was elected the Liberal Party split in two between the Lloyd George and Asquith Liberals, from which it has never recovered. My father supported Asquith and was appointed Liberal Chief Whip.

Bethnal Green was a curious electorate with a mixed population. It was close to the docks: London was the main port for the United Kingdom and a large number of dockworkers were employed there. These people voted Liberal prior to the rise of the Labour Party.

There were also the Huguenots who after 1685 had drifted to Bethnal Green when Louis XIV had expelled them from France. Many of these people were silk weavers. Some became street traders or costers and the flashiest dressers were known as the pearly kings, from their button-studded costumes. A Conservative government tried to drive them off the streets, but my father led a movement in the House of Commons which, despite the Conservative majority, withdrew this piece of legislation following massive demonstrations against it. This earned him the eternal gratitude of the costers.

Support for Labour was growing quickly after World War I and was led in the constituency by an ex-communist, Joe Vaughan. Meetings became very rowdy at election time when 'The Red Flag' was sung, and fights would take place. My father's meetings were always attended by a group of costers who wore their 'beetle crushers' and ganged up on known agitators, quickly subduing the protesters by stamping on their feet with their boots.

Another element in Bethnal Green at that time were the Jewish people, who all supported my father. They ran London's garment

PARENTS

Mrs Pankhurst's purple and green fan, given to Frieda Harris, depicts a Chinese scene.

industry known as the 'rag trade' and made lots of money. They have since shifted to Hampstead.

My father was created a baronet by Stanley Baldwin's Conservative government for his work for the people of London. He discovered that, as a baronet, he had to be of 'some place' and he chose Bethnal Green, and so when I inherited the title I became Baronet of Bethnal Green. He believed that the title would lose him support in his electorate, but quite the contrary. His electors felt very complimented and he received letters of congratulation from all over the electorate.

The rise of the suffragettes caused my father a lot of embarrassment, as my mother was an ardent suffragette. She was a close associate of Mrs Pankhurst who famously chained herself to the gates of parliament. Mrs Pankhurst left her fan to my mother and it is now in the possession of my daughter Margaret. Frieda would certainly have been jailed if my father had not been an MP.

Asquith was a vehement anti-feminist, perhaps because his wife Margot bullied him all his married life.

During the years of World War I, the country depended almost entirely for its survival on the work done by its women. After the war their demands became irresistible and forced the Lloyd George government to grant suffrage. Thus began their escape from the harem.

When World War I began, my father volunteered to join the army. Fortunately his short sight disqualified him. If he had got anywhere near the front line, he would have been killed. He would have made a frightful soldier! Early in the war he wrote a letter to *The Times* advocating a volunteer training corps. In all previous wars, fighting was the prerogative of the professional armed forces. Such a thing as compulsory service was not heard of. World War I was a very different war, as the public was soon to learn from bitter experience.

I do not know what part my father played, but as a member of parliament for Bethnal Green I am sure he did his best to help his constituents in the very unpleasant conditions which existed at the time. The front line was on the Channel and on a quiet day the guns could be heard. People forget that London was quite heavily bombed in World War I. A bomb fell through our London office but did not do much damage.

My father served as an MP till 1945. During World War II the Liberal Party was entitled to be represented in the War Cabinet. Sir Archibald Sinclair was leader of the Liberal Party and was therefore the one entitled to represent the party, but he lived in Caithness in the north of Scotland and was frequently absent as Minister of Air. My father usually represented him in his absence.

As representative of Bethnal Green, which suffered some of the worst of the bombing, my father was important to the government. He was also a member of the London County Council and an expert on London's special problems. The government relied on him quite a lot for information as to how the people of London were reacting to the very trying conditions in which they were living. The public was marvellous in the way they stood up to the bombing.

I was in London shortly after the war and saw something of the devastation, though it was not as bad as in Hamburg and Hanover.

I had an opportunity to compare these cities as well soon after the war. They were bombed flat. Even the gates of expensive homes were twisted into grotesque shapes. Hamburg was totally destroyed in a firestorm caused by the bombing.

Winston Churchill, then prime minister, made my father a privy councillor, and I believe he thoroughly deserved this honour granted to him for the work he had done for the people of London during World War II.

An election was called at the end of the war and Labour soundly defeated the Churchill government. The electorate was grateful to Churchill for his leadership during the war but believed that with the coming of peace it was time for a change.

Percy was one of the many who lost his seat to Labour and not long after that he lost his seat on the London County Council as well. Everyone believed that a new era would start with peace, but politicians remain politicians and alternative systems are much worse than democracy, so there was only a temporary swing to the left.

My father purchased a lovely old house in Chiswick on the mall opposite the river Thames. He had an assortment of old friends as neighbours, including Sir Michael Redgrave the actor, who lived next door, the writer A P Herbert (a parliamentary colleague), and George Belcher, the cartoonist, who was suspected of using my mother as one of his characters.

My mother had separated from my father some time earlier — theirs was a marriage of a couple that could not have been more ill-suited to each other. An Irish housekeeper looked after my father, and my brother and his wife shared his home for some time.

Percy became one of the local characters, as he was seen walking the streets of Chiswick with his little white dog. The fights of his dog with that of the president of the Garrick Club almost forced my brother to resign because they took place at the entrance to the Club!

Percy's clothes were rather old-fashioned (he wore button boots) and he was never without his bowler hat and umbrella. On one occasion he was waving his umbrella at a passing bus and when the bus stopped the driver called out: "'Ere comes the fairy queen!"

The great occasion in Chiswick was the ancient ritual of 'swan upping.' Unmarked swans in England belong to the crown and no one is allowed to kill them except with its authority. (In the Middle Ages, swan meat was regarded as a great delicacy). Swan upping consisted of marking each swan and cygnet with a sign of ownership, and clipping wings. People in Chiswick participated in this event to the best of their ability.

In one ceremony associated with swan upping for many years, the Vintners and Dyers Companies would drink a toast to the monarch after passing through the nearest lock to Windsor Castle, with the words: "His Majesty the King, Seigneur of the Swans."

One of the last official duties my father performed was as a member of a committee set up to select a suitable memorial for King George V. His friends told an amusing story about my father. Sir Percy asked one of the other members of the committee as to who that young man was with whom he had been conversing. His friend replied: "Don't you know who that is? It is the king." My father was very short-sighted and had not recognised him, and George VI was the last person to stand on protocol.

Unfortunately, George VI's health was very poor. He was a heavy smoker and died of lung cancer early in 1952.

Percy's health too had deteriorated rapidly and he died shortly after attending the king's funeral. The war years had taken a heavy toll on his constitution and, apart from his smoking, he had some strange ideas about diet. He was certainly not a drinker; a glass of sherry was the most he ever took. Despite having a rather violent temper, he was a warm-hearted man and was proud of his family. He had many friends in the political world on all sides of the House, including James Maxton who was believed to be a communist.

Percy's funeral at Westminster Abbey in 1952 was attended by all the high and mighty in the political world. I was unable to go because I could not leave New Zealand at that time for various reasons, but my brother represented the family. I do not know what my father's religion was as he never discussed the matter with me. In his last years, he was much courted by the Anglican vicar in Chiswick and attended church services quite often; he probably considered himself to be an Anglican.

Percy is buried in the Anglican cemetery at Chiswick with a suitable memorial designed by my mother.

When I was last in England I was asked by the Bethnal Green Council to unveil a plaque in the new council building. It was a glorious day and a moving ceremony to celebrate the life of a man who sincerely loved the people of Bethnal Green.

My mother

My mother, Frieda, was an interesting character. In accordance with Victorian tradition she was sent to a private school in Bourne End. Her teacher was the wife of Rudy Lehmann and mother of the famous poet, Rosamond Lehmann. Rudy Lehmann was a famous rowing coach and sent the first ladies' eight to Henley in which Frieda and her sister competed, attired in long skirts in case anyone should see their legs. I don't know who they rowed against but Frieda would wear a Leander scarf, much to my embarrassment.

When she was first married she was very social and did a lot of entertaining at her house in Sloane Square. She became an ardent Christian Scientist and as a child I was daily instructed in the works of Mary Baker Eddy. I suffered badly from tonsillitis and adenoids and had difficulty breathing. Instead of having them removed, I was prayed over by a Christian Science practitioner. The tonsils and adenoids were removed when I was sixteen and I have never had a day's sickness since. I have no love for Christian Scientists.

Frieda developed a desire to be an artist and went to art school. Her pictures were quite interesting but not quite good enough to achieve fame. When we were in Paris I suggested to her that she paint the scenes in the apartment. She did this and painted under the name of Jesus Chutney, achieving some notoriety.

She collected a number of artists as friends. I could have bought some paintings by names that later became famous, but could not afford to do so. Among her contacts was Aleister Crowley, in his time notorious as one of the world's bad men. He created a coven, which Frieda joined in her search for novelty. Members of the coven were undoubtedly given hallucinatory drugs. On one occasion it was agreed that Frieda had been turned into a frog and on another, she and other members of the coven danced on the cliffs at Dover to keep the Nazis away. I am sure Hitler was terrified and must have been frightened away as he did not arrive!

Crowley had the idea of writing a book about tarot cards and invited Frieda to do the illustrations. He was meticulous in insisting they were correct to the smallest detail and Frieda had to make many copies to correct minor mistakes. These tarot cards became standard for fortune telling. I had a number of copies and a signed copy of Crowley's book at Te Rama, but all were lost when the house burnt down. The originals are in a museum in Greenwich.

When I was in India, I went to see some Indian dancing. Later the dancer, Ram Gopal, and his team were performing in London and Frieda rushed around to introduce herself. She entangled herself with Gopal and helped finance him. She later followed him to India where he was helping to produce a film called *Elephant Walk*. She fell in love with India and bought a houseboat in Srinagar in Kashmir. She collected a boatman called Shaban who became her devoted servant. He would sleep on the floor outside her door in case he was needed, despite the fact he had a family in Srinagar. He learned to cook the awful milk puddings she liked, in addition to the fruit and vegetables which were grown on the floating islands on the lake.

When I visited Frieda, Shaban was careful that I should be protected against anything he considered unsuitable for a Sahib. Frieda was not permitted to introduce me to her guru. Shaban was a pious Muslim and I suspect he hated Hindus. On one occasion I visited a Hindu village in which there was a huge spring and a pool in the middle of a temple. Apparently this was a sacred area and I should have taken off my shoes. I was asked by a priest in perfect English to remove them and he invited me for tea. Shaban appeared from nowhere and with a horrified expression removed me.

Frieda was getting more and more eccentric and we were much embarrassed by her behaviour. On a short visit to England I remember on one occasion we lost her. I found her hanging onto the arm of a Marine outside the American Embassy. She returned to India and died shortly afterwards.

Frieda was psychic. When I first left for Australia she came to see me off on the ship. As I was about to go on board, she pointed out a party ahead and said: "That girl is your future wife." That girl, as it happens, became the mother of my children.

My wife and I later visited Kashmir and stayed in the houseboat, which was large and dank. One night, the houseboat next to ours sank in the middle of the night and some very charming English 'visitors' came aboard. We were much amused by dozens of Kashmiris trying to raise the boat by manpower.

Kashmir is very beautiful with lakes, high mountains and

Bronze of Frieda, sculpted by
Edward Bainbridge Copnall RA (1903-1973).

chestnut forests, the wood from which is used in furniture. It is floated down the rivers. Unfortunately, the climate is very variable. My wife caught pneumonia, which she could have died from, but fortunately we had some antibiotics with us. Shaban lit a huge fire to dry her out. Shaban himself later died of pneumonia.

In those days it was an attractive place for tourists but it was, and probably still is, full of drugs. An official, a very pleasant man who was on the lookout for drugs, visited us. Because of the ridiculous fighting over a bit of mountain, there are no more tourists and the place has to be maintained by the Indian government.

When we were staying there, we found Frieda had become some sort of saint and her portrait hung in the sitting room surrounded by flowers. She was buried in the Church of England cemetery but there was no headstone. So, we arranged a headstone to be placed over the grave containing the lines from *Cymbeline*:

Fear no more the heat o' the sun,
Nor the furious winter's rages;
Thou thy worldly work hast done,
Home art gone and ta'en thy wages.

It was a moving little ceremony, joined in by some of the locals. That night Frieda appeared to come and sit on my bed. Her appearance was very vivid and she said that she had come to thank me for remembering her.

III
My early life

I was born on 23 July 1906 at the family home in Paddington, London, and therefore I am a cockney, born within the sound of Bow Bells. St Mary Le Bow church is quite close to St Paul's and in those days (when noise came mostly from horses' hooves) it might just have been possible to hear those bells.

I can remember when there were very few cars in London; there were a few buses, mostly driven by steam. Electric light was just beginning and the streets were lit by gas, which was very effective in the thick fogs. After World War II, open fires, the main cause of fogs, were banned. Aeroplanes had just begun and there was no television or radio. My great treat was watching the silent black and white movies of Charlie Chaplin.

The following inventions did not exist: washing machines, electric stoves, refrigerators, radios, television, ready-made clothes, packaged biscuits, to name but a few. Travel was mainly by train.

Britannia really ruled the waves over an empire on which the sun never set, and foreigners were frogs or wogs.

I was a very badly behaved little boy, overweight and bad-tempered. When I screamed, Mother would hold a mirror over my face — this treatment was usually effective.

In accordance with Edwardian custom, my younger brother and I were left in the care of nannies. They always preferred my brother, who was better behaved. Perhaps my behaviour was caused by my tonsillitis. We moved around a good deal but before 1914 we lived at Hampstead in a house known as the 'Admiral's House' — it had been built by one of Nelson's admirals. The roof was constructed like a quarterdeck and the admiral would fire his guns to celebrate Nelson's victories. We were living in this house at the beginning of World War I but later moved, partly because of the noise of the anti-aircraft guns and partly because my father, as a member of parliament, had to live near the House of Commons. We moved to Queen Anne's Mansions, close to Victoria Station.

I was old enough to remember something of the conditions during World War I, but there are few people alive today who can. To a healthy young boy the shortage of food was very noticeable. Food was strictly rationed and we had to eat what we were given, which was enough to keep us healthy. The rich, of course, managed very nicely on the black market.

My mother and we children went to live on a poultry farm on Westerham Hill, which gave me an early experience of country life. During the period of hard rationing the farm was a treat as there were plenty of eggs and poultry and we made butter from cream in a large bowl.

Schoolboys were acutely aware of the war, as too many of their fathers were killed in action. In the streets the wounded and disabled wore a distinctive blue uniform and were also very noticeable. Surgery was not nearly as good as in World War II and there were many disabled, as well as those blinded by the gas attacks.

Just after the war my father took me to Normandy for a holiday. It was very awkward because I did not drink alcohol and even tea was difficult to obtain, and my favourite ginger beer was not available. Things like water closets were unknown at the time. There are, however, some wonderful old castles along the Seine, which we visited, but French was not my father's strong point and communication was difficult.

Winchelsea

When I was a boy, Grandfather Harris gave my mother a cottage in Winchelsea, which was one of the Cinque Ports. It had a huge unfinished church in which are buried some Crusaders. Winchelsea was abandoned as a port when the seabed rose, leaving nearly two miles of marshes between the sea and the old port. In the middle of the marshes is Camber Castle, quite derelict (though now being restored). It was built by Henry VIII in the 1530s.

You enter Winchelsea up a steep hill through some ancient gates and from the lookout you can see the shores of France, particularly at night. It was all very romantic and a suitable home for retired artists and writers.

Ellen Terry, the renowned actress, lived there and would organise performances by the locals of *A Midsummer Night's Dream*. I think this was the first time I saw Shakespeare performed. I was not then aware that Ellen Terry was the great-aunt of Sir John Gielgud.

Arnold Bennett the novelist lived there. He wrote the book about the Staffordshire Five Towns. My grandfather took me to see him and I remember him as a nice old gentleman with a broad accent.

Memories of my school days

I was sent to preparatory school in Shrewsbury when I was eight. I remember crying all night. I hated prep school and remember it chiefly for the number of times my bottom was beaten. Earlier, I had been at a school in Westgate called Street Court. There was a master called Creed who used to administer 'horse bites'.

Years later I was in Kenya and visited the golf club which still preserved the traditions of Victorian England. I was put through the usual questions: "Where were you at school? What university?" and so on. Finally I mentioned prep school and Street Court. One of the men announced that he had been there too and asked me if I remembered a man called Creed. He said he was terrified of him because of the horse bites, and had never really got over it. The headmaster also enjoyed beating the boys. I am afraid that I am made of somewhat tougher mettle and look back on my experiences with some amusement.

I had to struggle a little but passed the Common Entrance exam and landed in the third form at Shrewsbury School. Our housemaster did not believe in beating the boys. He would emerge occasionally and tell one of the prefects to castigate fellow pupils when necessary. Prefects were not encouraged to beat the younger boys and I was only beaten once very lightly. I admired our housemaster, an elderly bachelor. He had a passion for books and would attend the school library on Sundays to talk about the school's unique collection. I spent too much of my time there and neglected my studies.

Some of the masters were men who had been appointed to fill in during the war, and mine was one. Riots would break out in form time and the headmaster had to intervene. I showed no ability at games but loved rowing on the Severn, a beautiful river: I particularly enjoyed sculling up the upper reaches where one could also swim.

The school was completely segregated and girls only appeared with parents, and, as I had no sister, I was frightened of girls. Under these circumstances, there was, I believe, some homosexuality, but masters were too innocent to find out, indeed the word was

My early life

unmentionable. New boys were subjected to being called out by the prefects who shouted, "Scum!" The last boy out was usually me so I had to do the odd jobs.

It was usual for one of the younger boys to be elected for a year as Hall Crier. When I had the honour (or dishonour) I had to get to my feet and announce anything that was lost in the House and say, "Oyez, oyez, this is to say God save the Queen and down with the Radicals." I was the obvious choice as the son of a Liberal MP; there were no Labour MPs in those days. I succeeded in making a joke of the whole thing and made quite a lot of friends at school. I did not like school, but I did not dislike it.

I made some little effort and managed to pass my university entrance exam and went to Trinity Hall, Cambridge.

Cambridge

I really enjoyed my time at Cambridge. I was not a success at sport but joined in every university activity, and was president of the College Literary Society for one year. Through my father I arranged some interesting literary speakers, including the poet Walter de la Mare, the historian and travel writer Philip Guedalla, and poet Edith Sitwell, a strange person. Later on both she and my mother lived for a time at the Ladies' Club, and both were turned out: Sitwell for getting drunk and Frieda for waving her stick at the staff and insulting them.

My second year was marked by the General Strike of 1926. We all enlisted as special constables and went up to London where we drove around the city in a convoy. We had free seats at the theatre and were entertained everywhere. I had no feeling against the strikers and realised there was a good deal to be said for them. It was a little embarrassing when we all landed up at my father's electorate. I think my father supported the strikers.

I demonstrated in their favour by reading the *Workers' Weekly* in the police station. Politically, I supported my father, rather tepidly, but I was also an ardent pacifist. This was before the rise of Hitler, which changed everything. My greatest friend, Nicholas, was an ardent Conservative. I was a little surprised when I met him later in London to find that he was working for the Labour Party.

I developed my great interest in history at Cambridge and obtained a reasonable degree in history and economics. Without a knowledge of economics it is very dangerous to run a business. Anybody who doesn't understand economics really doesn't know what's going on. I was interested, and there was a funny thing too about this degree. When I went up to Cambridge, we were taught the classic idea of supply and demand — when demand went up, the price went up. Then a man called Henry Ford came along and when he started to manufacture cars the price went down. It made nonsense of the whole teaching. But as it so happened, in my last year at Cambridge I had Maynard Keynes as a lecturer, and he reversed the whole thing. Keynes's thinking had a huge influence on everyone who studied economics, which led, for instance, to the decision to abandon the Gold Standard.

Learning about business

Boys who left school were expected to go into the armed services or one of the professions or lead the life of the idle rich. My father very much wanted me to go into the law. If you were intending to study law you had to go to the Inner Temple and have dinner at a table which was headed by a senior legal man, and the idea was that they'd look you over. So I used to go to town to 'eat the dinners' at the Inner Temple. In those days the theory of the legal profession was a little different to what it is now. It was not how much law you knew, but how suitable you were to become a lawyer, and this was the place where you were deemed to be acceptable or not.

But I wasn't interested in the law, I wanted to go into the business. That was something I got from my grandfather who had run the business almost to the day he died. I think I was much more like him than my father in character.

My father wasn't pleased with my decision, but he was very good about it. I didn't know a thing, so he tried to get me a bit of education about business. But he hadn't much idea and there was no such thing as business school at that time. He went to Morleys, a big merchant house in London, and asked them to take me but they wouldn't. However, the joke was on them, because they went out of business before Bing Harris!

In France at the couturier's

When I came down from Cambridge, my father arranged for me to go to France and Germany.

My mother had a friend who was a French couturier, so my father decided to send me to work in this business. He seemed to remember vaguely that Bing Harris had something to do with women's clothes, so I found myself in a women's fashion establishment in the heart of Paris. Fortunately, I had learned a little French when vacationing in my student days with a French family, who as it happened spoke no English.

I don't think the firm knew quite what to do with me. My father probably paid the owner to pay me a small salary, but I was quite useless. Anyway, as the couturier business consists of pinching ideas from each other, I was sat down at a table in a corner and left to take cuttings of other people's designs from fashion magazines. The place was full of mannequins and I was absolutely terrified at being with all these strange women. I had a romantic idea that it would be wonderful to have a beautiful French mistress, but this did not eventuate. I was far too shy to approach any of the girls at work and was also a bit of a snob about any who might have obliged.

I was very lucky with the place that I lived in. I had a friend who was an artist and he had a flat in Rue de Vaugirard, where a lot of artists lived. I didn't know him well, but there was some sort of Jewish connection with my family, and he let me have his flat and went off to England. Along with his flat came his 'bonne', a cross between a servant and a housekeeper, who looked after me and used to buy the most enormous quantities of butter. I remember this because butter was quite expensive in France.

Paris was a stimulating place to be at that time. All the great French artists were around, some of whom I met through my mother when she came over to stay with me. It was at that time that she began painting pictures under the name of Jesus Chutney.

During this stay I developed a taste for French modern art and French food. I found home very 'English' — roast beef, Yorkshire pudding and plenty of stodgy puddings!

Visit to Germany

After my six months in France, my father had the idea that Germany was the place for me to learn about business, and in 1928 he sent me to Berlin to learn a little German.

He gave me an introduction to a bank with which he had some connection, but had no idea that Berlin had the reputation for being the most immoral city in the world. The bank manager recommended me to a German count by the name of Von Becker. The spectacle I saw there was an eye-opener to me. Count von Becker and his male friend were busy arguing about the boyfriend they shared and what clothes they should buy for him. Fortunately for me, I have no homosexual inclinations and found these activities funny.

I visited the granddaughters of Johann Strauss, the famous composer. One of them, the younger, I found very attractive. I was so unsophisticated I thought I had to ask both of them out, and my courtship did not get very far, although they did notice and remark that I was not a homosexual. Practically all the nightclubs were homosexual and it was very embarrassing to go there by oneself. Fortunately there were also concerts and marvellous opera. There was the beginning of the German movie industry with stars such as Marlene Dietrich. There was also great art developed by such as Marc Chagall, Max Ernst and Kandinsky. All would later be driven out of Germany or killed by Hitler.

I lived in several boarding houses during this time, and this gave me an opportunity to meet young German contemporaries. Most of those I met spoke quite good English but I could not speak German well at that stage.

It was a lonely place for me. The winter was bitterly cold and on Christmas Day everything was closed and a freezing wind blew snow down the wide streets. It was cold enough to turn the snow into powder. After about three months I transferred to Hamburg, which was not as forbidding a city as Berlin, and I got to know a young man called Sir Richard Powell with whom I used to visit the nightclubs. Fortunately, I was too shy to approach the tarts.

It was still freezing and I would walk across to the small office owned by the company's shipping agent. I don't know what I was supposed to do there except learn German from the newspapers.

During my visit there were interesting political developments going on, with the rise of the Nazi Party. They wore brown shirts and the communists wore red. I saw the beginning of the anti-Jewish campaign. My friend Powell and I had a friend who was an Austrian count but also Jewish. The owner of a shop spotted he was Jewish and tried to throw him out and we came to his rescue and did some minor damage. We went back to apologise to the owner who was very pleasant and had not suspected my possible taint.

I found there was a lot of bitterness against the former Allies but particularly the French, because they had made exorbitant demands for reparations. The German economy was denuded of all overseas assets to enable it to meet the French demand enforced by the occupying French troops. Because of these demands, inflation soared and the Deutschmark became valueless except possibly as lavatory paper. The lifetime savings of the middle classes were destroyed: some of the wealthy sections of the community wiped off all their debts while assets remained intact.

The large shops, particularly in Berlin, nearly all belonged to Jews — they came in for obvious anti-Semitism. Non-Jewish firms such as Krupps also benefited; their armament industry was intact and ready to take advantage of the rearmament programmes started when Hitler came into power supported by the Nazis.

To make matters worse, at the time of the peace negotiations, the Chancellor of Germany was a Jew. Hindenberg and Ludendorf exploited this by alleging that the Treaty of Versailles was a conspiracy by the Jews and that if it had not been for this the German army would have gone on to victory, although possibly at the cost of many lives. This was an obvious lie because the increasing number of American forces arriving in Europe at that time defeated Germany. Some Germans also blamed their government for failing to resist the demands of the French.

All this was a wonderful opportunity for Hitler, whose oratory whipped up support for his plans, which led through from increasing oppression to the ultimate Holocaust. What I believe is not generally remembered is that these events also benefited the communists! Clashes took place between the Nazis and the communists in which the Nazis were not always successful.

When I arrived home from my stay there, I told my friends

that we would be at war with Germany in a few years. No one believed me.

I met one or two former members of the German armed forces and they put forward the idea that Germany and Britain should get together and attack Russia, after which they would dominate the western world. I pointed out that I did not believe that this idea would appeal to the British. I think that the delay in attacking the British army was because the Germans still had that dream and did not want to destroy it.

Bing Harris warehouse (second building from left),
Maclaggan St, Dunedin, 1862.

IV
Bing Harris 1858–1929

Before I tell the story of coming to live in New Zealand, I should perhaps give some background to the firm in which I played a leading part over almost fifty years.

The history of Bing Harris dates back to the early settlement of this country, and I think the fact that my grandfather was chairman of the company from 1858 nearly until his death in 1926 and I was chairman from 1935 to 1979 must be a most unusual record in the history of New Zealand.

The early history of the company must, therefore, be of some interest to New Zealanders who study the background of those pioneers who arrived here at the time the country was first settled by Europeans. Much emphasis in the past has been given to those who settled on the land, but life would have been intolerable for them without the services provided by the merchant houses which brought into the country almost all the necessities of life and distributed them throughout the country through the small general stores, often financed by the merchants who, in turn, provided credit for the farmers.

People today cannot imagine the difficulties which existed in pioneer times bringing goods to the men who were opening up the land or mining the gold in the rugged terrain of Central Otago.

There were no roads or railways and goods had to be carried either on horseback or in buggies on half-formed tracks subject to destruction by floods or burial by snow.

Dunedin and Auckland were the first commercial centres of importance in New Zealand. The stimulus to the growth of Dunedin was the discovery of gold in Central Otago and settlers arrived in large numbers as the news spread to Australia that strikes were rich. Dunedin developed from a town of huts to a city very much as it is today in the years 1868–71.

In Gabriel's Gully thousands of people were staking claims. Some of them struck it rich and some did not but, as far as I can find out, most of them lost their money either gambling or in the pubs, except for a few Chinese families still resident in Dunedin.

Dunedin was fortunate in that it also attracted men of ability and vision. Most of the large commercial houses were founded in Dunedin in the 1860s and 1870s; many others were merged or taken over or virtually abandoned by families who had made their fortunes and settled in England.

It is hard for people today to realise the isolation of New Zealand in the early days when communication with the rest of the world was by sailing ship and entertainment was only in the hotels and in private homes.

Even when I arrived here from London in 1929 the isolation of this country and the lack of knowledge of the rest of the world struck me forcibly. England was 'home' and many people's ambition was to go there and have their family educated in that country. In such circumstances roots and local loyalties were not formed here, more particularly by the business community, for whom it was easier to turn their assets into cash than those who had invested in land.

Among those who arrived in New Zealand was my grandfather, Wolf Harris, some time in the mid-1850s. He commenced importing goods from Melbourne and after two years had collected sufficient funds to return to Australia where he purchased more substantial quantities of goods. Unfortunately, on his return to New Zealand the ship carrying him and his stock was shipwrecked off the Taranaki coast and all was lost. He used to tell a story that they had to hide in a cave to avoid hostile Maori raiders.

His credit, however, was good and he was able to purchase more goods from the merchants in Melbourne and start again in business. His first premises were in Maclaggan Street in Dunedin, not much more than a storeroom.

In 1858 a partnership was arranged with a Mr Bing, when he bought out a Mr Turnbull who had been Bing's partner. Mr Bing proved to be an unreliable partner and during a trip to Europe he overstayed and failed to carry out his commissions. My grandfather consulted his bankers, the Union Bank of Australia, and they had sufficient confidence in his ability to advance him, without security, enough money to enable him to buy out Mr Bing as well, but the name of the firm remained Bing Harris.

In those days there was little or no manufacturing in New Zealand and practically everything other than home-grown meat and vegetables was imported from England. The success of any business, therefore, depended upon its ability to select merchandise suitable for the market and to arrange shipment for distribution this end. In 1871 my grandfather married Elizabeth Nathan and it was not long after this that they took up residence in London where he attended to the buying, at which he demonstrated a great deal of ability. An arrangement was reached with L D Nathan in Auckland by which their London buying was done by Bing Harris, and Nathans kept out of the rest of the country and Bings kept out of Auckland.

The business in New Zealand was managed by a series of partners who were bought out on retirement. This arrangement worked out successfully for a time because of the ability of the first two New Zealand partners. My grandfather used to visit New Zealand periodically, quite an undertaking in those days, but as he grew older he became more dictatorial and less in touch with what was going on in New Zealand.

It is as well to remember that, although practically all the importing was carried out by merchants or middlemen, there was a larger number of them, and the population of New Zealand was much smaller than it is at present — I do not think it was ever more than one million at any stage in the 19th century. Consumer demand was also on a much lower scale than today, and wages were much lower even allowing for the cost of living adjustments. A young man would be glad to start work for five shillings a week and anyone earning £400 per year was regarded as quite wealthy. Indeed, there was not much to spend money on. As a matter of interest, in 1932, just before I became managing director, my salary was £400 per annum.

In the 19th century, few of the amenities of modern living were available, no motor cars, only the beginning of a railway service, no electric light, washing machines, radio or television. The few wealthy people built large houses, employed servants and tried to emulate the customs usually associated with prosperous living in 19th-century England. The ambition of all was to make enough money to retire to England and enjoy their prosperity in that country, rather than adapting themselves to the way of life which was developing in the country where they had made their fortune.

Although the firm had a good reputation, in its capital and trade it was small compared with today's ideas of a substantial business. In the year ended 31 March 1903, for instance, sales were £299,513, stock at the end of the season was £113,209, gross profit £48,336, nett income £14,716. Those who are interested in modern business procedures will note the very satisfactory stock turnover which was a consistent feature of a period of years.

During the previous century the business must have been that much smaller and the problems of management were nothing like they are today. Indeed business was on a very leisured scale. Country customers were provided with drinks when they arrived at the warehouse and the same procedure was expected in country towns when the general traveller arrived with his dray. The boss, of course, went off to a five-course lunch at his club, ending up with brandy and cigars.

Correspondence that was lost later in a fire showed that Wolf Harris endeavoured to exercise a tight control over the business from London. The problems of implementing his ideas must have been overwhelming when one considers that correspondence was by sea mail, taking six weeks or longer from port to port.

Despite the excellence of Grandfather's judgment when it came to buying, it appears that the standard of performance of the next two partners were the reverse of satisfactory. One appears to have been an alcoholic and the other a thief. Furthermore, my grandfather had very definite ideas as to the functions of a wholesale merchant. In his view, the activities of the firm were to import merchandise from overseas and sell the goods to the retail. Attempts to develop manufacturing activities were frowned on, and even a suggestion that the old warehouse in Dunedin, built in 1861, should be pulled down and a new building erected with retail shops in front was vetoed.

The simplistic approach to the operation of the business had its merits as the firm seems to have had a pretty consistent record of profits for a long period, but the steady development of New Zealand manufacturing from the 1920s reduced the market for imported goods, whilst the retail trade which had formerly been in the hands of numerous small traders tended to fall into the hands of large groups, a trend that has accelerated to the domination by retail chains in recent years.

Early in the 20th century Leslie Harris, my uncle, was sent to New Zealand to run the New Zealand end of the business. Again, I had correspondence from those times that showed him arriving here full of enthusiasm, and he would probably have made a success of things if he had been given a chance.

Leslie Harris was an agreeable young man of an easygoing disposition. Nevertheless, the records demonstrated that during his early years in New Zealand he did take a great interest in the business and made some constructive suggestions. His father, however, was evidently a papa of the best Victorian tradition and all proposals were turned down, and he even raised the kind of objections to his son's marriage which would have been put forward by Edward Barrett of Wimpole Street fame.

It was only a matter of time before Leslie became discouraged and spent less time in this country, until after World War I he took up permanent residence in England. As I mentioned, my father also spent a short time in New Zealand before I was born, but neither he nor his wife liked this country and they quickly returned to England where my father entered politics.

The situation therefore developed that the owners of the business were entirely resident in England. They occupied intermittently a dusty Victorian office on the ground floor and basement of 8 Philip Lane from which they issued an incessant stream of good advice to the management in New Zealand who, I suspect, took not the least notice of it.

Grandfather, who was becoming an old man, had by then given up attending to the buying and it was left in the hands of men with little knowledge of New Zealand requirements and, particularly in the apparel field, they were often sold inferior goods.

The management of the business was left in the hands of three men, Mr W Lees, chairman and Wellington manager, Mr Gerald Benson, Dunedin manager, and Mr C Trimnell, Christchurch manager. The local chairman, Mr Lees, was an accountant who knew only how to say no; he missed opportunities and ground the business down.

Gerald Benson came to New Zealand in 1902 as manager of the manchester department and later became Dunedin manager. He was a well trained warehouseman and devoted to the interests of the business. He trained the staff thoroughly in business procedures, and without his enthusiasm the firm would not have survived the long period of neglect from after the war to 1935. He was very conservative in his ideas and we had many disagreements after I took charge of the business in 1935, these disagreements sometimes developing into violent arguments at board meetings.

In all these circumstances it is not surprising that the fortunes of the firm began to crumble. It was saved from collapse by the advent of World War I. New Zealand was mainly dependent on imports from Britain at that time, supplies were hard to obtain, but having a London office proved a great advantage and it appears as if price controls did not exist. Unfortunately, the buyers were so eager to obtain supplies that they placed orders for delivery as soon as possible. By the year 1920 supplies began to catch up with demand and in 1921 disaster struck all the major wholesale houses in this country, all of whom had adopted similar practices.

British manufacturers looked through their order books for orders which had been placed four to five years earlier and goods began to arrive at wartime prices which were substantially ahead of current market prices. British manufacturers were adamant that they had firm orders and did not care about the embarrassment they caused their customers. My grandfather had to offer suppliers up to 30% off the price to persuade them to cancel their orders.

Sir David Ewen of Sargoods told me that as a young man he had the same experience with his company.

In the year 1921 the firm lost half its capital and all the reserves built up in the war years; it survived because my grandfather made available his private fortune as a guarantee to the bank.

In 1926 he died, aged 93. Until the last few years of his life he had actively controlled the business, although he became increasingly out of touch with changes which took place in New Zealand and lack of contact with the staff he employed. He was, in fact, totally dependent on managers whose activities he had little knowledge of or control over. He made the mistake of failing to place sufficient authority in the hands of his sons and he would not let them make their own decisions, so that as they grew older they lost interest.

I have seen this happen with so many businesses — Ross & Glendining, perhaps in its time the most successful wholesale and manufacturing company in this country, was for many years run by a Mr Jeavons in Dunedin and a Mr Miller in Auckland. They trained no successor and it was not long before this successful business was in trouble and was wound up.

In the following few years the firm recovered to the extent of making modest profits but it was in no condition to deal with the effects of the Depression which began in 1929 and lasted for at least five years. This is Bing Harris as it was when I became involved with the company.

Bing Harris traveller, Alexandra, Central Otago, 1905.

V
Starting life in New Zealand

After I returned to England from Germany, I spent a short time in the London office of Bing Harris. All correspondence was by codes in cable — pantelegraphy it was called — and I was chiefly engaged in decoding cables and going for trips with the buyers. At that time most purchases for the New Zealand operation of Bing Harris were made through London.

I had formed the ambition of going to New Zealand fairly early in my life. I used to talk to my grandfather and my grandmother. They had memories, and pictures and photographs, and they had books. I was particularly interested in *The Long White Cloud* by William Pember Reeves. I was influenced from an early age by them, though my father and uncle rather sat on them when they wanted to talk about New Zealand.

So I had made up my mind to go to New Zealand. I thought I might be able to rescue the neglected family business and I liked the idea of open spaces, mountains and volcanoes.

A lingering look back

Before I refer to my life after I left England, I would like to say a few words about how I remember it more than seventy years ago. Before motor cars became so common, the country was beautiful in the spring with its flowers. The hedges were full of sweet-smelling flowers such as violets and primroses. There were bluebells in all the woods and cowslips in the fields. The fumes from traffic have poisoned all the flowers along the country roads. In the summer, meadows were a glory of poppies and cornflowers. These have been destroyed by chemical sprays. The roads are now so congested that it is almost impossible to drive out of London at the weekends, and privatised railways have produced chaos, as well as being very expensive. Even the Underground is dirty and overcrowded. One thing I am certain about is that I do not want to live in England again.

England was a very pleasant place for the privileged, and the tradition of being a gentleman was still important. On the whole, working people were polite and friendly, although it was no joke being unemployed.

As a visitor, I have found things much changed. Many of the young people are rude and undisciplined. One only has to see what happens at the soccer matches to realise this. They are unhelpful to the elderly, unlike in Australia, where the public is more than kind to old people. Of course I realise that many things are better than they were. For instance, social security does protect the underprivileged. When I used to drive around the country I noticed the huge estates that occupied most of the land were devoted to protecting pheasants and animals such as foxes. These estates have been turned into farms now, whilst the great homes are open to the public or owned by institutions.

An incident occurred while I was in England. I visited Apsley House, the London residence of the Duke of Wellington at Hyde Park Corner, to see again how the house looked at the time of Wellington, but found, to my disappointment, that it had been changed around. Later, I met the duke in the Wellington Club. I told him that I missed the large nude statue of Napoleon that had stood in the entrance hall. He said, "You would never believe what happened in an air raid during the war. A piece of shrapnel flew through the window and neatly deprived poor Napoleon of his penis."

En route to New Zealand

My father booked me a first-class ticket to Australia on the Orient liner *Orontes* in 1929. To me, everything was both romantic and luxurious. A steward would lay out my dinner jacket every night and I would dine at the captain's table. This was not altogether an advantage, as I had to be punctual for dinner and be on my best behaviour.

It was on this trip that I was fortunate to meet my wife, Patricia Penman, the young woman whom my mother had pointed out to me on the day of our departure. She was only nineteen and there is something romantic about going out on deck with a pretty girl. We must have begun to fall in love with each other because it was about three years later that we married.

I always remember when I first met my future father-in-law. He drew me aside and said with a twinkle in his eye, "You can hardly believe this. I was talking with someone aboard ship who said, 'You cannot be associated with that man, he is a business wallah'."

We called at Colombo, which was still a British colony at peace with the world and I took Pat out to dinner for the first time. The next day we went to the beach and had a great swim. I remember one instance; there was a snake charmer. To my surprise, he spoke perfect English, probably educated in England. I asked him whether he had any personal contact with the cobras. He replied that this was not possible. He mesmerized them with his pipe and his hands.

Sydney was still quite a small city — less than a million inhabitants, and life was centred around the Rocks and the Domain. I was introduced to my future wife's home at Wahroonga. The harbour bridge was not yet built and we crossed the harbour by ferry. The Penman home was very attractive with a large garden and swimming pool and tennis court. I actually saw oranges growing for the first time!

Wellington in 1929

I travelled on to New Zealand on an ancient Union Company ship called *Makura*, a bit of a let-down after the romance of the *Orontes*. The trip took about four days and I arrived in Wellington with a howling black nor'westerly blowing and no friends or relations to meet me.

My first encounter with New Zealand was a sad disillusionment. Wellington in those days was a very depressing sight. It consisted of rows of shabby wooden buildings with corrugated iron roofs interspersed with a few Victorian horror brick buildings faced with plaster, and nothing had been painted for years. Rattling old open-sided trams crawled down Lambton Quay. You could not get a drink after 6pm except with dinner in one of the few hotels. You had to be in for dinner before 7pm, where you were served a rather English-style meal by forbidding waitresses dressed like hospital nurses. There were no restaurants other than fish and chip shops and only one modern building, the DIC building, which was shown off with great pride by the locals. The only social life was around one or two cabarets where the locals used to hide their bottles under the table or the ladies' skirts when the police arrived on the scene.

There was no television, and contact with the outside world was by ship or cable. Even radio and 'talkies', as films were called then, were in their infancy. Visits by J C Williamson's theatrical companies were the highlight of the year.

Things might have been easier for me if I had been a sporting type, but I would go for long walks, sometimes by myself. I did know some people. Fortunately, it had been the custom for the locals to send their sons to Trinity Hall in Cambridge, where I had gone myself. Leonard Tripp, the family lawyer, recommended the college to his friends. I was put up at the Wellington Club by Phil Brandon, whose father had been the president, and lived there until I found accommodation.

I was interested to find the Maori produced some wonderful carved artifacts with sharpened stones. There are plentiful supplies of jade, known locally as greenstone, from which ornaments and weapons are made. The Maori people are good artists and write interesting books and have some fine musicians and I found them to be very friendly people and have yet to meet one I disliked. I estimate that within 50 years they may be completely integrated; it is already very difficult to tell who is Maori and who is Pakeha.

In 1929 there were no diplomatic representatives, and members of parliament did not often visit Europe. The first British High Commissioner, Harry Battersby, arrived following the appointment of a number of consuls from other countries and gradually Wellington became less isolated. When the Germans invaded Czechoslovakia in 1938 one of the diplomats, a friend of mine, was summoned to meet the prime minister who wanted to ask him, "Where is Czechoslovakia and what is it?" He could not resist telling me about this.

I was welcomed up to Government House by the Governor-General, Lord Bledisloe, on my arrival. It took some time for them to discover that I was the son of the first Sir Percy Harris and they made a great fuss of me. Then they discovered that they had confused my father with another Sir Percy Harris. This other Sir Percy Harris later arrived in New Zealand and I got to know him quite well.

Early days with Bing Harris

Of all the depressing places I visited in Wellington I think the old Bing Harris warehouse was almost the worst. The square grey building was decorated with concrete bobbles on the roof. They fell off in a subsequent earthquake and it was almost as if they had been placed there with lethal intentions! Inside, the building had not had a coat of paint in years. It was lit by open light bulbs and merchandise was piled on long counters. Customers were invited to look through the stock, and often left an almighty mess behind which had to be tidied.

Senior staff consisted mainly of a number of dear old gentlemen, relics of the Victorian age. They certainly had no idea of marketing, and the selection of goods was, in the main, from samples which had been sent out by the London office. Management and office staff sat in tiny offices from which it took many years for me to escape. I was regarded as somewhat of an embarrassment and left to look round. However, shortly after I arrived, the manager announced his intention of going for a trip to England and left me in charge at the age of twenty-four. I had virtually no business training, a poor staff, a Depression on my hands, and a princely salary of £400. I shall never forget my experiences during the next few months, I appealed for help to Mr Lees, the former manager, but he was just not interested. My accountant was a Mr Junk who was more interested in converting the heathen than in looking after the accounts.

What help I received was from Gerald Benson in Dunedin but I think he rather resented my arrival. I had a number of offers from people to sell our goods, because jobs were hard to obtain in the Depression. I remember an elderly gentleman with side-whiskers who told me that he could sell the goods and would show the young men what an energetic old chap could do. He did make sales, but to every crummy account and hawker in the North Island and we were never paid.

It soon became known that Bings was an easy take and these gentlemen descended in droves on the warehouse as they realised that our accountant was thinking about heaven and not earth. Fortunately, one or two of the senior staff knew their business and so not all was lost through bad debts and jobbing.

I would like to briefly mention one practice: every year buyers from certain stores would travel round the country, inspect the old stocks carried by the warehouses and offer to buy at half cost price. During the Depression these gentlemen made fortunes out of our bad judgement, but the policy of quitting stocks at the end of the season did keep down our investment in stock which would otherwise have accumulated and would have quickly put us out of business. The accumulation of old stocks is the kiss of death to any firm involved in the apparel business and it is the primary duty of all management to see that this does not occur.

Dunedin, 1930

When the Wellington manager returned I was sent round the country and spent some time in Dunedin where Gerald Benson presided over what life there was in the old firm. The staff there were if anything older than the Wellington staff. An elderly gentleman by the name of Mr Portman, who had a large walrus moustache and the appearance of Old Bill, sat in a high chair in the office writing out the accounts in longhand. He used to wear a flat cap and ride home on a bicycle, and was one of the well known sights in Dunedin. At least the warehouse was efficiently managed and I learnt the basis of my training in that city.

If Wellington was a dump, Dunedin was something worse, presided over by the Presbyterian Church. Sunday was reserved for religious services; I think you were allowed to play golf in the afternoons. Beach guards made sure that men's bathing costumes were not rolled down and lipstick was frowned on for women. Subjects suitable for conversation consisted of (for men) rugby football, of which I knew nothing, and the price of wool. For women, conversations around the children and whom they would marry were considered suitable topics. Fortunately, among the young there was an active social life. Parents had a way of going off to England and then the parties really started! One of the Sargoods had married a man called Mills. They named their home 'Piccadilly' and it became the centre of much social life.

Shortly after I arrived in New Zealand George Milne, my mother's nephew, also reached this country, and for many years he and I ran the business. He was first employed by the millinery department in Dunedin; later he went to Christchurch as shipping clerk.

After a time I returned to Wellington but again was not given firm employment, although I was appointed a director in 1931. I was, therefore, a director of the company for forty-eight years.

The business continued to make losses and it became evident that sooner or later the bank would tire of supporting us and would put in a liquidator, unless it could be proved that some positive action was being taken.

I wrote repeatedly to my father and uncle suggesting that one of them should come to New Zealand and do something about it. They were joint governing directors, and as they also owned all the shares they could have done what they liked. Neither of them would budge. My father used to write to tell me to wind the business up as it was an old man of the sea, in which case there would have been precious little for the shareholders, but this did not seem to worry him. My uncle took a slightly different line, he would write each year and say triumphantly that he had told us we would make a loss and now we had made one. He would then add constructively that we must be careful and not spend too much money.

It was clear that no one intended to do anything until the bank stepped in.

In the meantime I had married Patricia Penman from Sydney and had a family to support, so things were pretty desperate for me. Finally I took matters into my own hands and went to see the Wellington manager of the Union Bank as it was then, and explained to him that the owners of the business were quite unwilling to take any positive steps, that I was aware that the business was going bankrupt and that I wished to do something about it before it was too late.

Mr Porter was a good banker and took me upstairs to see the general manager, at that time a Mr Fotheringham. I had several interviews with this very understanding gentleman of whom I have the warmest memory, and finally he invited me to run the business and said that the bank would support me. He added that he had a friend, Jack Griffin, who had just completed a big job for the bank in Australia and that he might be prepared to act as a consultant and serve on our board.

I met Jack Griffin and he was asked to prepare a full report on the business, which he completed in his usual thorough way. If the report had been unfavourable I am sure that the business would have been placed in the hands of a liquidator, presumably, J L Griffin. However, he recommended that the bank continue to support the company and that I be given a chance to put things right, with his assistance.

Shortly after this he joined the board of Bing Harris & Co Ltd and remained a director until 1968. He was joint governing director with myself from 1944 until his retirement. His wise counsel was invaluable to me and the board as a whole, particularly so because for many years he was the only non-executive director of the company. He would sometimes sit through long boring meetings and would make only one or two remarks, always to the point. On occasions we would be unable to decide what was the right thing to do and would agree to differ. Jack would turn to me with a twinkle in his eye and say "that has fixed it." It is, perhaps, a tribute to us both that during our long years of association all decisions reached by the board were unanimous.

During the early days of our association I would call on him at Clarke Menzies to discuss my problems about once a week, and I certainly needed all the advice he could give me.

The situation the company faced was a difficult one. About half the capital had been lost and all its reserves, and the company was deeply in debt to the bank which held a mortgage of all its assets.

The two most important jobs were, therefore, to reduce the stocks and collect the book debts, many of which, particularly in Wellington, were bad or doubtful. The first thing which had to be done was to introduce a tight system of budgetary control of all buying.

Fortunately for me the worst problems of the business centred in Wellington, where the branch had been thoroughly badly managed. I had, therefore, to retire the manager and fire the accountant. I brought Mr C N Fraser to Wellington from Christchurch where he was the branch accountant, and he became company secretary and branch accountant, with the balance sheet prepared by the auditors. George Milne came to Wellington, where he was for a short time shipping clerk, and then took charge of the women's outerwear which he ran successfully until he was called up early in the war. Returning later he became a director and I managed the Wellington branch as well as attending to my other duties.

Incidentally, when I was appointed chairman and managing director I was paid the princely salary of £1,100 per annum plus £150 director's fees. I was provided with neither a car nor an expense allowance and I had a wife and child to keep.

It was indeed true that only through exercising the most rigid economy could the business hope to survive.

The branch managers and I were deeply involved in all the activities of the business. All planning and buying was supervised by one or other of the executive directors and I don't think there was even a letter opened except under the supervision of a director. Our executive directors may have been too deeply involved in the day-to-day operations of the business but they knew everything that was going on. In Wellington all correspondence passed over my desk before it was posted.

Patricia

Patricia's background was completely different to mine. She was born in Cobar, in the heart of New South Wales, and her father was the manager of the great Cobar copper mine.

When she was young she could mirror-write. She had a flair for acting and had an early stage career, helped enormously by her remarkable memory — she could memorise her lines without difficulty. She

Patricia Harris, 1970s.

was a great homemaker and designed two wonderful homes for the family. She published three books on cooking and entertaining — *Dining In and Dining Out in New Zealand*, *Fit for a Sultan* and *Accept with Pleasure* — and fed me far too well. She had a long association with the Plunket Society and was Lower Hutt president 1945–1954, and later patron of the Abortion Law Reform Association of New Zealand. She was a contributor to the *New Zealand Herald* and the *Listener*, a broadcaster, poet, feminist and civil libertarian. We had a great collection of books, china and red glass, which sadly was lost in the fire — a great blow to both of us.

We had a wonderful marriage together and never had any fights. We would have friendly arguments from time to time — we were so completely opposite and so completely well suited. I loved her and she loved me until the day she died.

Our social life in the early days

We were married in 1933. Patricia had left her lovely home in Sydney to come to New Zealand where I had nowhere to live. We first went to Dunedin where we lived for a while in a hotel, which actually had a fireplace. There was no central heating. She would sit in the Botanic Gardens' greenhouse to try to keep warm. Later on my father-in-law and his wife came over to visit us. We went to Queenstown and the Hermitage, where it snowed heavily. I don't think she had seen snow before.

She must have loved me dearly to join me in New Zealand where I was running a half-bankrupt business. Later on we were able to build a nice home in Woburn Road in Lower Hutt, which was where we had our three children: Christopher John Ashford Harris, Margaret Suzanne Ashford Harris, and Paul Percy Ashford Harris.

meet the family ...

MEMOIRS OF A CENTURY: SIR JACK HARRIS

Christopher was born in 1936 and went to boarding school at St Georges, Wanganui. Later at Wanganui Collegiate he excelled at swimming and running. When he left school he came to work for Bing Harris, and went on to make a career in finance. He has three children: Andrew, Charlotte and Phoebe. Andrew has a daughter, Madeleine, and Phoebe has three children.

Margaret was born in 1939. She came to England with Paul, Nanny, her mother and me in 1951 for almost a year. On return to New Zealand she went to Nga Tawa School, Marton, then to art school in London. She had a son there, but came home and ran a riding school here for 30 years. After selling the school she took up art again, among other pursuits. Through Barnados she made contact with her son, Matthew Taylor, who to our astonishment has been in the House of Commons since he was 22 for the Liberal Democrats — and has the same rooms in the House of Commons that his great-grandfather Percy had.

One of the most interesting parts of our 1951 visit to England was a six-week trip around post-war Europe in an enormous Humber Super Snipe, into which we put five of us: me, Patricia, Margaret, my father Percy and Patricia's mother Doris, not to mention all our baggage. We started in Sweden at an international Liberal conference where Percy was a speaker, then drove through Denmark to Hamburg, which was still devastated after the war. In Italy we stayed a week or so on an island in the middle of Lake Garda, Sirmioni, then went to Switzerland and France.

Paul, born in 1945, went to St Peter's, Cambridge, where he was head boy, then to Wanganui Collegiate, where he was successful all round. He went to Trinity Hall at Cambridge University where his grandfather, Percy Harris and I had been. Paul married Gail, who he met at Cambridge, and went to Sydney where he works as a stockbroker. He has four children: Mark, Sophie, Nick and Sam.

VI

Depression, the first Labour government, and war

In 1929, shortly after I arrived in New Zealand, the Great Depression began in the USA with the crash of the stockmarket. The Depression lasted as long as it did because the Bank of England clung to the idea of the Gold Standard, so that all gold held in Britain and elsewhere drifted into Fort Knox in the United States. Consequently there was no money left to buy anything. It took some time for Britain to realise that this was the cause of the trouble. It also took a long time to get it right.

In 1931 New Zealand was governed by a coalition of the Reform Party (led by Gordon Coates) and United Party (led by George William Forbes). The government had a fine solution — and that was to do nothing at all! In fact, since the time of Richard Seddon nothing had been done to improve social conditions. There were no public works, no housing construction and no encouragement for local industry to develop. There was unemployment on a grand scale and the unemployed were largely left to fend for themselves. People were starving. On one occasion there were riots in the streets of Wellington and farmers were brought in from the country to break up the riots with stockwhips.

The country was in a mess. Britain realised that New Zealand was going to the pack and they sent out a man called Ted Fussell to set up the Reserve Bank. Later on Sir Harry Battersby was sent out as the first High Commissioner. Britain had no representation in New Zealand before his appointment. Things began to open up a little bit once Sir Harry arrived.

New Zealand was so completely isolated. Nobody knew anything that was going on in the outside world. What finally really opened it up to commerce was the arrival of commercial aircraft — this was the brainwave of Charles Kingsford-Smith. We met him at the St George Hotel in Wellington in 1936. Patricia and I brought our eldest son (a baby at the time) to meet him and he sat on Kingsford-Smith's knee! Smithy had piercing blue eyes and I found him a most interesting character. Unquestionably the airline that later assisted in opening up the markets was Qantas Airlines.

At the end of 1935 there was a general election at which the Coates/Forbes government was handsomely defeated by Labour. If ever a government deserved defeat it was this one. I can well remember Michael Savage's election campaign. He had a soapy voice and a mournful manner; he had a capacity for reducing his audience to tears.

This was the first Labour government and most of those who had not supported that party believed that this was the beginning of nationalisation of production, distribution and exchange in accordance with traditional socialist doctrines. As it turned out, their philosophy was conservative compared with many right-wing governments today in that they believed in balancing their budgets and severely limited their overseas borrowing.

The government almost immediately embarked on an extensive policy of public works, in particular a massive scheme for the building of state houses. It was interesting to note that they tried to buy out Fletchers, the only people in the country who had the ability to construct houses in bulk. They were able to capitalise on the planting of hundreds of square miles of pine trees in the centre of the North Island, from which we continue to benefit today.

As prices for our primary produce continued to be low it was not long before the government ran short of overseas funds. Partly to protect these and partly to foster secondary industry, a detailed system of import licensing was introduced.

As I had placed tight control on all buying, this created an embarrassing situation for Bing Harris because entitlement was based on past performance. Controls at the time were so rigid, however, that we were able to sell anything we could import as well as getting rid of our old stocks.

It began also to be possible to apply for special licences and this duty was placed in the competent hands of George Milne. I think we gained some advantage over our competitors in that these applications were always handled by a senior officer of the company whilst our competitors left them in the hands of their shipping clerks.

It became clear that we must try to enter manufacturing if we were to survive. My grandfather had always resisted the attempt by local management to develop manufacturing and had insisted on the disposal of our clothing and footwear factories in Dunedin. The clothing factory was, I think, sold to Sargoods. None of my directors had any experience of manufacturing, and our financial resources were such that we had very limited funds available for this purpose.

Our first venture was the manufacture of ladies' outerwear. A representative of a German clothing manufacturer had recently arrived in New Zealand with a range. As he was a German Jew he became stranded through the rise of the Nazi party. I approached him to suggest that he manage a clothing factory which we called

Bond Street Models Ltd. To obtain the necessary import licences we had to register this as a separate company.

We obtained the services of the smartest models available and took them to the Department of Industries & Commerce to present our most attractive dresses. Apparently their officers were suitably impressed and we were able to obtain the necessary import licences.

The manager, Mr Rosen, proved to have a certain amount of ability although this was sheer luck as he had no manufacturing experience, but he did understand women's clothes and was successful in manipulating staff. We were also lucky in obtaining a designer with a good knowledge of fashion. It was not long after this that war broke out. Good quality ladies' clothes became unobtainable and during the war years this little business made good profits.

World War II

Shortly after the beginning of the war Prime Minister Michael Joseph Savage died. He was regarded as a saint by the working people and as a communist by those that didn't agree with him. When he died there was an outpouring of grief throughout New Zealand. Peter Fraser, who succeeded him, was a dour Scot who had come out to New Zealand to work on the waterfront. He didn't work; he used to sit in the lavatory and read! The result was that when he finally became prime minister he was very well educated. He is best remembered for his achievements as Minister of Education and as prime minister during the war.

Early in the war, staff at Bing Harris began to be called up to the armed forces and it became difficult to handle what goods were available. Fortunately, in the South Island our staff was rather elderly but in Wellington I had replaced some of the senior staff and we faced some pretty severe difficulties. I relied to a great extent on Charles Fraser, who was a branch accountant as well as company secretary.

During the war years a different sort of problem developed. Almost anything could be sold and it was a question of obtaining supplies. Bing Harris had a good deal of success thanks to our London office. It is hard for people to realise today how dependent this country was on imports from Britain and the Continent.

The manufacturing phenomenon in the Asian countries did not exist, although there were some textiles available from India. Our access to the American market, our only other source of supply, was not particularly good. Manufacturing in New Zealand, other than the woollen mills, was in its infancy.

I was fortunate not to be called up because of my age and two children. However, I joined the Volunteer Reserve (later called the Home Guard), and we used to prowl around the Lower Hutt area armed with ancient rifles for training purposes. It was supposed to be a morale booster at a time when things were going very badly for the Allies. When Japan entered the war we were sent to defend the coast with our ancient weapons. I was given a hand grenade which I was supposed to throw. I was quite terrified at the thought and escaped the task. The peculiarities of the Lewis gun also eluded me. It was clear that soldiering was not my thing. I was surprised to find that some of my fellows were illiterates: they thought the army was fine, no need to think at all. What was better than standing there doing nothing? I hated sentry duty; my problem was to keep awake.

An opportunity arose to join the Security Intelligence Bureau (SIB), which had been set up to protect New Zealand from saboteurs. A man called Major Kenneth Folkes was sent out from Britain to run the show. He spent most of his time chasing women and the rest of the time fighting the police, which was difficult for those who worked for him. It was ironic that he was ultimately replaced by the chief of police.

The job suited me well. Practically all my staff, apart from some aged men, had been called up for military service. I would slip around the corner to run the office and someone would call me if I was needed. I do not know how the firm would have survived without this. At one stage I even had to run the accounts, but had a very competent lady to assist me.

Some of the security staff emerged dressed in full captain's uniform. Apparently this was done to impress some of the Japanese who had revolted in the prisoner of war camp in 1943. I remained a sergeant.

There was not much to do except to deal with letters. One confirmed that Mrs So and So was a German spy because she cheated at croquet, and there were numerous reports of people signalling out of their windows to German ships. A man who called himself Captain Calder announced that he had unravelled a plot to kill Peter Fraser. The boys at the top of the SIB had a wonderful time travelling all over New Zealand looking for the supposed assassin. If they had spoken to the police they would have discovered that there were no assassins. The whole thing was a plot dreamed up by a well-known con man, but they did not check him out.

I was employed in boarding the ships arriving from overseas. They were usually captained by men born in Germany, but what could be done about that? We had a list of suspects, but I do not remember apprehending any undesirable persons, except an engineer who had set fire to the engine room because he thought it was being sabotaged by dolphins. He was drunk on eau de cologne. Apart from this, I would be sent across Cook Strait in small fishing boats to prevent the Italian owners from contacting submarines or entering forbidden areas, which they always wanted to do because that was where the best fishing was. They were a cheerful lot and fed me on good Italian food. I did not like to go down below for a rest because I did not know whom I might share a bunk with.

On one occasion on a hot day I became very tired, and, driving home, went to sleep at the wheel and crashed into a power pole outside the power station, setting off air raid sirens in the Hutt Valley. As far as I know this was the only air raid warning that went off in New Zealand during the entire war!

When I was on night duty I would breakfast at the Wellington Club. Often Gordon Coates, who was Minister of Armed Services and War Co-ordination, would be there. It caused me some amusement having breakfast with the Minister of Armed Services when I was only a sergeant in security. In May 1943, on a cold morning, I moved over so as Coates could sit near the fire as he was feeling the cold — I returned to the bureau and two hours later learned that he was dead. Coates was a congenial character who enjoyed life and was an ideal contact for the first American ambassador.

There was a story about Coates going with the ambassador to watch American troops make a trial landing on Kapiti Island. The commander of each landing craft was announced, and each had German names. Coates put up with this for a while, but finally he said, "Come on, let's run — Hitler's landed!"

The great earthquake of 1942

Just about the time of Pearl Harbour, we experienced the great earthquake of 1942. We lived in Lower Hutt and you could hear the rocks rumbling down the valley. Soon our beds began to slide up and down the room. My wife was just beginning to recover from pneumonia at the time of the earthquake. I would not allow her to leave the room or take the children outside as it was too dangerous and this particular night was very cold.

The architect Bernard Johns had designed the house. It was built on 'rockers' and this allowed the building to move, absorbing some of the shock of an earthquake. Although the chimneys of other houses in the valley were badly damaged, the only damage I experienced was the loss of one ornament.

VII

People, politics, and events in Europe between the wars

Lloyd George

In 1916, during World War I, David Lloyd George replaced HH Asquith as prime minister, just as later in World War II Winston Churchill replaced Neville Chamberlain. Asquith, the leader of my father's Liberal Party, was totally unsuited to be a war leader: he was also suspected of being pro-German because he had German relations, but then, so did the king — the allegations of being pro-German were, of course, totally untrue.

My father had a lot to do with Lloyd George, who was a dynamic leader in war, prepared to overrule the armed forces when he considered it necessary. From a very different social background to Winston Churchill, he was originally a small-time country lawyer in Wales, but unlike Winston, he spent a lot of his time chasing the ladies. I have heard him speak — he had a golden voice and was a natural orator. Both men were the men 'of their time' able to lead their country to victory.

When the war was over, Lloyd George formed a coalition government, which was dominated by the Tories (Conservatives) as they were then known. Asquith regarded Lloyd George as a deserter and led a small team of Liberals into opposition to the government. My father was appointed Chief Whip of this group and it was not long before the Tories realised that they had had enough of Lloyd George in the biggest possible way, and forced him to resign.

The Liberals were by no means overjoyed at taking Lloyd George back into the fold. He became an independent member of the party, however, and they could not have survived without his help.

While Lloyd George was prime minister he was in the position to grant honours to his supporters. While some were undoubtedly earned, others were sold at a scaled price in accordance with the importance of the honour granted. The money was placed into a fighting fund for the Liberal Party, but Lloyd George had complete control of it. The fund totalled about £1,000,000, a lot of money in those days. My father had the thankless task of visiting Lloyd George, who had retreated to the country, to try and extract money from him. Apart from the difficulties he experienced in obtaining money from Lloyd George, whose actions as a member of parliament were quite unpredictable, he began to cause real embarrassment with the rise of Hitler.

Lloyd George was invited by Hitler to visit Germany. He was given royal treatment by Hitler and was much flattered by this attention. When he arrived back in London he announced his admiration for Hitler, which caused much embarrassment to the Liberal Party because the Jewish community largely dominated it.

On the other hand, because they were obsessed with the danger of communism, the Conservative Party at that time actively supported the Nazis. I can remember Neville Chamberlain, when he returned from Berlin, having a piece of paper in his hand: 'Peace in our time'.

The British government condoned the rape of Czechoslovakia and it was not until the invasion of Poland that they realised that they had clasped a viper to their bosom. The Conservatives asked Neville Chamberlain to resign, replacing him with Winston Churchill as prime minister.

My father, because he was a Jew, was heavily courted by the Jewish community, but seemed to be totally uninterested in what was being inflicted on his people by the Germans: he always felt he was English not Jewish and did not wish to become involved.

My brother and I got to know the Lloyd George family, who were all charming and intelligent — we never met the eldest son. He disapproved of his father's amorous affairs and resented the treatment of his mother, who was a well-loved person.

The build-up to World War II

Most English people were anti-communist but the Conservative Party, which was in power at that time, was particularly anti-communist and believed that the Nazi government would prevent the continued expansion of communism in Europe.

After occupying the Ruhr without much opposition from France (which had a weak government at that time, headed by Blum) Hitler then demanded the return to Germany of the Sudetenland (German-speaking people). Perhaps he had a case, but the world was becoming nervous about what Hitler intended to do next.

Russia offered to join the West in an endeavour to stop Hitler, and they might perhaps have succeeded. The British and French governments decided not to agree to this proposal. Later on, Churchill named Chamberlain and Halifax as appeasers. It does not seem to have occurred to anyone that they had a point. It was assumed by the West that in the event of Hitler's defeat, democratic government would have returned to power.

My observation in Germany at that time forced me to reach a different conclusion. The Communist Party was certainly the second strongest organisation in Germany at that time, and I believe that they would have seized power. The communists would have then dominated Europe as far as the Rhine.

The communists in Russia under Stalin's leadership were very aggressive and anxious to spread their regimes as far as possible. It seemed to me that they would continue their advance over the rest of Europe. Strong communist parties already existed at that time and I do not believe that Western Europe would have offered much resistance, so what would have happened to Britain? There was even a communist party there.

It was a horrible shock to the British people when Hitler marched into Poland. The British and French governments had made commitments to protect Poland but I do not think they realised they were going to be asked to meet them so soon. When information leaked through of the atrocities being committed in that country they began at last to realise what they were up against.

Even after all this, the appeasers, particularly Chamberlain and Halifax, still believed they could negotiate with Hitler, forgetting that Hitler described the treaty he signed with Chamberlain as "a scrap of paper".

Winston Churchill

Winston Churchill was a courageous man and was dismayed at the idea of surrendering without a fight. Churchill became prime minister when this crisis occurred and with his genius for passionate oratory persuaded the British public to back him.

They did not realise how hopeless the situation looked, but the escape from Dunkirk rallied them behind Churchill and the entire country was put on alert. There was some delay while the Germans were preparing their assault. By a superhuman effort, Britain built enough fighter aircraft to drive the Germans back and provide further time for re-armament.

In the meantime, the British people, with some passive help from the USA, continued to resist the Germans alone. Hitler then made a great strategic mistake when he ordered the attack on Russia before demolishing Britain, which would have taken place inevitably in the long run. The Germans thought that the Russian defence would collapse within a few days, but they were mistaken and their victories were reversed at the heroic defence of Stalingrad. Without this resistance, there is still a doubt as to whether victory would have been achieved if the Russian government had surrendered, but it was this heroic defence of the country which enabled the successful landing of the Allied troops to take place later on in the war.

I shudder to think what would have happened to Britain if Germany had won: a Quisling type of government would have been put in and pogroms would have taken place. Winston would have been the first to die, although I am sure he would have died fighting. My father, as deputy leader of the Liberal Party, was high on the hit list. He was also a Jew and would probably have been tortured and murdered.

I think, however, that Hitler would have been defeated in the long run, probably somewhere in the heart of Siberia or elsewhere. He was an ignorant man and had not learnt the lessons of Napoleon and Alexander the Great. These men did make an attempt to conciliate the conquered indigenous populations, but Hitler inflicted the worst violence on all the populations of the countries he conquered and antagonised all.

I believe that without Winston's determination and courage Britain could not have retained its independence.

As a student of history I had spent time studying Winston's personality. My father was close to Winston: he was at school with him at Harrow and, as described earlier, served from time to time in the War Cabinet. Winston often told my father that he (Winston) was a liberal, and I think this was true. As a young man his views were even radical. After World War I he even suggested that profits beyond the first £10,000 should be taken from war profiteers in the form of taxes. In his old age, in his last spell as prime minister, he strongly pushed for the payment of a proper living salary to MPs.

Before he became prime minister, Churchill depended largely on his own resources and was successful in doing this due to his own prodigious output, originally through journalism and later by writing books. His life of the first Duke of Marlborough alone ran into three volumes. By this effort he managed to achieve his standard of living, but he worked far into the night to achieve this. He was brought up in the extravagant way of life still practised at the time of Edward VII and was determined to maintain it, which he did.

In addition to these activities, he went to enormous trouble to prepare his speeches; they were seldom spontaneous. It is said that he practised important speeches in front of a mirror. He must have had an amazing constitution to have lived to the age of 85, as he was never without his cigar, ate voraciously and drank a great deal. He stayed faithful to his wife, which helped greatly.

When he became prime minister, and due to circumstances that existed at the time, he was able to do much as he pleased — the country could not have done without him. He never spared himself and took terrible risks on his travels: he was fortunate indeed, and so was the country, not to have been killed by the Germans. He did have a 'double', which confused them: the prize to the Germans of killing him would have been very great.

On his travels Winston was always accompanied by a large staff and expected to be entertained royally wherever he went. He had a fine contempt for rationing. He felt that the country owed it to him, and perhaps it did. As time went by he tended more and more to neglect the advice of his staff, and this may have contributed to the mistakes he made later in the war.

Another failure of his was that he was much influenced by flattery and particularly lavish entertaining. An instance of this was his relations with Stalin. Stalin wanted desperately to influence him to open an early front in the West to relieve the German pressure on Russia. This would certainly have proved disastrous; fortunately Churchill resisted this and was backed by the Americans.

Nevertheless, he was completely deceived by Stalin's attention and on several occasions went to consult Stalin about the conduct of the war. The worst instance occurred later on, when the Russian prisoners who had escaped to England were sent back to Russia and promptly murdered or sent to a concentration camp. Anthony Eden was always blamed for this but he could not have acted without Churchill's consent. I believe the bombing of Dresden was also carried out to impress Stalin.

Trouble arose for Winston when the Japanese entered the war. In New Zealand and Australia the quick collapse and fall of Singapore was blamed on the failure of the top defence officials to co-ordinate the various branches of defence, and for a general lack of realization of the implications of the fall of Singapore by the British government. The impression was that it was a long way away and did not really matter much to Britain.

The attitude of Churchill to what he regarded as the colonies became plain when he wished to send Australian forces to Burma at a time when the Japanese threatened their home with invasion. The determination of the prime minister of Australia, John Curtin, prevented this happening and Australia was saved.

Similarly, he failed to understand the strong desire of India for independence, which caused a minority of Indians to support the Japanese in preference to defending their own country.

The truth is that Winston Churchill was influenced by his aristocratic background, and growing up during the reign of Victoria made him a dedicated royalist. I think that he really believed that the colonies had a duty to provide soldiers to defend England at whatever cost. Non-white races under the British Crown had been taught that they were inferior to the white men, particularly those of northern blood, and with their unquestioned loyalty to the Crown they were there to be exploited by Britain.

Churchill was a truly great man and the world should be eternally grateful to him for his courage, which rallied the people of Britain behind him to the courageous defence of the British Isles.

His personality was unique in history, but like all great men he had his weaknesses. He must be judged by his great achievement as a wartime leader and by his contributions to literature.

Edward and Mrs Simpson

I left England in 1929 and was out of touch with British politics for a while. Patricia and I returned for a visit in 1936, just as the scandal over King Edward VIII and Wally Simpson was reaching a climax. We were given up-to-date information by my father, who represented the Liberals on the committee set up by the government to decide how to deal with the crisis caused by the king's stubborn insistence that he be allowed to marry Wally and have her crowned queen.

Such a step was quite unacceptable, as the Church would not recognise the remarriage of a divorced woman while her ex-husband (or ex-husbands, in Wally's case) was still alive — but it was far worse than that. Wally's pro-German sympathies were well known within the circle of the political élite in London.

It was widely believed that Hitler would invade England (successfully of course) which would enable Edward to regain his throne, subject to the whims of Hitler, who had already proposed a 'hit list' of persons who should have priority in the process of extermination — a list that included my father.

Stanley Baldwin was prime minister of Britain at the time and was a very worried man as he did not wish to be responsible for the fall of the monarch, and it was only as the crisis developed that he realised that the king's brother and his wife made a suitable alternative. Things were complicated by the loud noises made by Winston Churchill, an ardent monarchist who firmly believed that the king could do no wrong. I do not know what line he would have taken if Edward had still been king in 1940 and had expressed pro-Nazi sympathies then. Fortunately Edward VIII abdicated in 1936.

In the months before the abdication we were kept up to date on events by Percy, who came home with daily reports, particularly on aspects of the king's sex life. Percy claimed that Wally was the only person who could assist in 'getting it up'.

In the meantime, the king's behaviour continued to deteriorate. He would be seen about London with Wally and Joachim von Ribbentrop, the fanatical Nazi ambassador who once greeted the king with "Heil Hitler!" (*Punch* called him Von Brickendrop.)

My father arranged for Patricia to attend the only opening of parliament by the king, who was obviously drunk. In those days, there were, fortunately, no Murdochs and the press had been persuaded to keep quiet about what was going on. However, talk was inevitable around London and the crowd booed the king when he was driven past on his way to the opening of parliament.

When I returned to Australia and New Zealand, I found that

not a word had leaked out there about the troubles of the monarch, and men who should have known better accused me of being disloyal.

I was not in England during World War II as I was a permanent resident in New Zealand. Therefore I had to rely on my brother for first-hand news about England, but he was in the navy and did not know much about what was going on in wider circles.

VIII

Bing Harris — after the war to 1979

Shortly after the defeat of Germany, Bing Harris's company secretary, Charles Fraser, had an severe heart attack and was not expected to live. He was told by his doctor that he must retire, though actually he lived for another fifteen years. I managed to obtain release from my army service (with the Security Intelligence Bureau) and, until I found a new company secretary, I had to run the Wellington branch and act as company secretary and was chairman as well.

Fortunately, it was a matter of obtaining supplies rather than selling them. Goods were in short supply and the main problem was trying to maintain the goodwill of our customers with what goods were available.

After the defeat of Japan, members of our staff who had fought in the war began to return, and we were able to find jobs for all of them. I must add that all these men proved to be very valuable members of the staff. The discipline and experience overseas made them excellent employees; in particular, they always carried out instructions meticulously and did not mind hard work. Among them, George Milne returned from service in the Pacific and became a director. Sam McLernon came to us from Wilberfoss Harden as company secretary and later managed the Christchurch branch and became a director.

By the end of the war we had paid off our overdraft and were in credit with the bank, which enabled us at last to think of expanding the business. The government, both Labour and National, instead of removing wartime controls tightened them up. It was only under pressure that they were persuaded to remove petrol rationing long after it had become unnecessary.

In the 1950s Dr Sutch became head of the Department of Trade and Industry and government was very influenced by his theories, which were very socialistic. He envisaged a self-contained New Zealand which manufactured everything possible in this country, all industry to be protected by an insurmountable barrier of import licensing, and jobs would be freed for everyone. The idea behind all of this was that anything that could possibly be made should be made here in New Zealand. They went to ridiculous lengths to achieve this. For instance, Bing Harris had to import towelling in large pieces, cut it up and deliver the finished towels; of course, it cost more to do it that way than to import the ready-made towels in the first place.

Sutch's ideas were quite unsound, particularly for a country so dependent on exports, creating as they did a number of wholly inefficient industries as well as shortages of labour, which placed huge power in the hands of the unions. You cannot believe the number of restrictions that were introduced. There was almost nothing in the country that wasn't controlled in some way or other. The prices were controlled, imports were controlled, bringing in money into the country was controlled, and permits of every sort were created.

In such circumstances, if we wished to survive we had no alternative but to manufacture for ourselves as many products as we were able to in our own factories, which were on a very small scale at that time. To obtain the necessary raw materials for these factories, we were able to obtain import licences. Initially most of our fabrics came from England, but George Milne went to Japan where, I think, we were the first importers from that market. He also established contacts in the USA and Canada and I opened up contacts in India and Hong Kong.

Shortly after the war Mr Rosen, who ran Bond Street Models, returned to Germany with his wife, who had never adjusted herself to conditions in this country. We acquired a similar small business manufacturing ladies' coats and skirts by the name of Ethel May Mantles Ltd. It was in the same building as Bond Street Models Ltd and was owned by an enormously fat cockney Jew who used to say that you will make your money out of cabbage — the correct word is 'garbage', which is what you call the over-recovery you make on fabrics. This business also did reasonably well until the heated motor car destroyed the trade in ladies' coats.

Our next major operation was a factory called Chilco in Wanganui, which concentrated chiefly on children's wear and later on women's frocks. It was not a very efficient factory, but employed, at one time, a staff of about 150. Labour was cheap and partly Polynesian and Maori, but things became difficult for this factory when there was some competition and the unions moved in with restrictive practices.

To follow this, we started a clothing factory in New Plymouth which specialised in Guardsman sports coats. In Christchurch we had a factory manufacturing boys' shorts and girls' school blouses, and a joint venture manufacturing knitwear and a small factory making men's boots. In Levin we bought a factory which manufactured interlock underwear and T-shirts. In Palmerston North we had a joint venture manufacturing children's wear and bobby socks.

We then bought a firm in Auckland called Rainster. This seemed all right but no sooner had we done this when school children gave up this style of stiff raincoat. This is a hazard of the rag trade.

Bing Harris centenary celebration gathering, 1958. Keith Holyoake seated centre, next to Christopher Harris; Patricia and Jack seated far right.

Bing Harris centenary celebration: Jack and Patricia on left.

Bing Harris centenary — joint celebration with Bing Harris's long-standing shipping partner, Shaw Savill & Albion.

Bing Harris head office front entrance, with traveller's car, corner Willeston and Victoria Streets, Wellington, about 1960.

We inherited a Mr Pinker, who was a fundamentalist Christian. The leader of his church forbade the sharing of meals with non-fundamentalists and businessmen. Mr Pinker liked whisky, so he would retire behind a screen and have his whisky while we were left to have our drinks without him.

He continued the business by manufacturing skirts and jackets, a rather risky business which we entered into inadvertently. In the end, we merged the business and did quite well out of selling the properties.

We then went in as joint owners with NZ Forest Products and acquired a half interest in the supply of motor accessories. We built a large factory in Auckland and acquired a firm manufacturing specialist parts in Nelson.

At the time Bing Harris was sold to Brierleys the motor accessories venture was quite prosperous, but I did not follow the progress of this business and, of course, Forest Products was also bought out.

At this time we had altogether about 1500 employees and were one of the largest employers in the country. We also took over Macky Logan's. This was a good buy as it gave us another foothold in Auckland and some very experienced staff. I believe it was sold only because there was no one who wanted to run the business, just as it was with Bings when I came along.

Investor in Bings

Bowaters bought a block of shares in Bings and I did not know why the managing director came to see me — I took him round the company and showed him the Onehunga Woollen Mills, which we inherited from Sargoods. They specialised in manufacturing heavy woollen blankets, which no one was ever going to want in the modern world. On top of this, he promptly retired.

I contacted one of our suppliers in England and he recommended a man who ran a woollen mill in Ethiopia; but the needs and conditions of Ethiopia are far distant from ours. He was absolutely useless. I asked the people why the Onehunga Mills did not pay any more but I did not become involved with their negotiations. I subsequently selected a man from Mosgiel. He was a good manager but had no idea about marketing; he stayed with the company until after it was sold.

I then appointed a bright man who installed a spinning plant. He was ambitious and wanted to install a whole number of other machines: by then we had established a market for rugs. I pointed out to him that we had shareholders to look after: he promptly resigned, leaving me once again holding the baby. However, the business had become profitable and I had enquiries from people who were interested. Fortunately, Brierleys had taken an interest in the company by then and much of the decision-making was taken out of my hands.

Sargoods

George Milne's wife was one of the Ewen family who ran Sargoods and he learnt that they were not doing well. It was, therefore, to his advantage to promote Sargoods to Bing Harris. Negotiations took place through the medium of Bowaters, whereby Bings would buy the family out and pay each of the Ewen family a sum of money. George Milne represented the Sargood family.

George owned a property in Wanaka and announced his intention to plant a vineyard there. To those who read this story and are not New Zealanders, Wanaka is in the South Island of New Zealand. It is inland and subject to considerable frosts in the winter. I suppose the climate is not much different to that of the Rhineland. His friends thought that he was mad, but they were quite wrong. He made a huge success of the vineyards and Wanaka is now one of the centres of the wine-growing industry.

The Ewens were like many other owners of old family businesses, such as my father and uncle — they were the victims of inherited wealth and did not possess the necessary motive to drive a successful business in order to live well. Anyone who could make any sort of case would be provided with a car; anyone, similarly, could go on a business trip overseas. They did not appear to have any budgeting control over expenditure and they had not worked out a cashflow system.

It was not at all surprising that the firm was losing money and I had the unenviable task of cleaning up the mess. George was too involved in the other side to be effective. The idea was also put around by the Ewens that Sargoods had taken over Bings, which was quite untrue.

It was surprising indeed, though, that Bing Harris, a firm that had been nearly bankrupt about 25 years earlier was now the only general wholesaler left in the country, for which I take a good deal of the credit!

Unfortunately, there was another problem waiting in the wings. Business in New Zealand was rapidly being taken over by chain stores, and the merchant houses had become redundant in the Western world. I had the problem of dealing with this. My board did not have any ideas on this subject — muggins me!

There were really only two choices: to go retail, or wind the business up. I seriously considered going retail. This would not have been too difficult; but with a chairman about 70 years of age and about to retire, the board made a decision to wind the business up. I believe Brierleys intended to wind us up, although they did not say so.

I reached the age of 70 years in 1976 and it seemed to me that it was time I retired after 43 years as managing director.

I appointed Graham Valentine to replace me as chairman. In normal circumstances it is not a good idea to have the chairman and managing director as the same person. Unfortunately, Graham Valentine had no idea of the complicated way I ran the business.

Each of our subsidiaries had two or more Bing Harris directors, mostly myself and George, later my son Christopher. The first thing Graham did was to insist that all Bing Harris directors resign from the subsidiaries even when they were only partly owned — but then who would be responsible for running the businesses without directors?

Finally, when Brierleys offered to buy us out at $1 a share, which the board thought a bit low, they waited outside expecting to be called back. They were not. Christopher was pleased to come back to negotiate a better deal but Graham did not manage to do so.

Brierley Investments acquired Bing Harris Sargood in 1981 and it was broken up in 1984.

Brierleys asked me to stay on but I had had more than enough. I went off to make a new life with my wife, but did not expect to be still around 30-plus years later!

My wife and I were given a 12-month trip around the world by the board. I had looked after the interests of my staff but not my own. They had a profit-sharing scheme, a retirement policy and an opportunity to acquire shares. In return, my staff was very loyal to me. When I meet any of my former employees in the street, they always seem pleased to see me.

At the end of the Bing Harris era.

IX

Scenes from the East

Japan — 1947

I visited Japan on business not long after the war and found these people friendly and reliable to do business with; they adhere to contracts while the Chinese will try to get out of contracts if it suits them.

Shortly after the war the first post-war ambassador arrived in New Zealand and I was invited to meet him and say a few words on behalf of the business community in New Zealand. I reminded our guests that during World War I they were our allies, and probably would be again! My remarks met with a favourable response.

When we visited Japan some time later we were offered hospitality by the minister, who had by this time returned to Japan with his American-born wife. She invited us to her house, but this was not according to Japanese custom, so we were taken to a well-known restaurant accompanied by the New Zealand trade commissioner. During the evening one of the Japanese hosts pushed rudely past the commissioner's wife and my Japanese friend elbowed him so that he fell in the water, to my delight! Because of this, my friend lost his appointment but he was not without his own resources.

George Milne, my deputy and cousin, decided to visit Japan to open up business there. He contacted the government to obtain a permit and was, I believe, the first non-official to visit the country. He contacted one of the leading companies in Japan, Nishoiwai, and during this exchange laboriously translated his address: after he had listened to all of this the Japanese official replied in English! The Japanese love a joke.

George Milne was a large, heavy man and decided to hire a rickshaw — cars were rare in Japan then as they had not manufactured cars at that time. The rickshaw man started to go up a hill and then let go of the rickshaw — of course it fell backwards into a shell hole and poor George was covered with mud. He did not reveal this story because he thought everyone would laugh at him, which they did!

As a result of this visit, the trade with New Zealand logs was opened up and our company obtained the Nissho agency for the logs. Later on, when they were established in New Zealand they terminated the agency.

On my visit to Japan I was met at the airport by the chairman, Mr Nishikawa. I had brought with me a Kashmir ring scarf, which means that the wool was so fine that it would pass through a ring. Patricia had not liked it, so I gave it to Mrs Nishikawa. I did not realise at the time that it is the custom for everyone to give presents; it gave me a flying start as she was delighted. I then met the full board of the company who all seemed to speak English and we had a very civil reception. We were then invited to attend a party given by the company on our behalf. Token presents were exchanged, and I was allocated someone who I had already met in New Zealand to look after us during our visit. My escort liked to give us the impression that he was able to make decisions, but this was not the case. Everything had to be referred to the board. The question of face is very important to the Japanese.

Mr Nishikawa invited us to a geisha party, where my wife was a great success. She had a small nose and dark eyes — the Japanese are rather frightened of large noses and blue eyes. At 10pm we were sent home and they got up to their usual games.

In Japan, all hospitality must be returned, so a return party was arranged for us. What I did not realise was both parties were being charged against the commissions we had earned!

We visited the island of Kyushu where the atomic bomb was dropped on Nagasaki — curiously enough, the harbour was improved by its increased depth.

We also visited Madame Butterfly's home, where she lived after marrying her Japanese friend with whom she had two daughters. The house was a very comfortable home, not particularly Japanese in style. It escaped the bomb because it was on the hill. I walked through the town and found the people friendly, not hostile as I had anticipated — perhaps they were being polite.

Foreigners were often unaware that there were any monkeys living in Japan, a fact that most Japanese were unaware of too. They are very spoilt creatures and steal everything including your pocketbook if you are not careful. In my usual way I travelled around the country, which looks like the North Island of New Zealand, but the vegetation is different. There are snakes in Japan. There are shrines everywhere, which are obviously revered.

Japan is even more volcanic than New Zealand and there are hot springs everywhere to bathe in. You are not allowed to wear clothes and the water is very hot — one is expected to have a massage after bathing.

Japan was isolated until the 19th century but they are an adaptable people and quickly saw the advantages of the modern technical civilization, and adapted themselves to modern technology. But they still held to their traditional customs when I was there and were not influenced by Western ways. Why should they be? We could learn a great deal from them about behaviour.

Visit to China in 1978

Chairman Mao was a different sort of dictator to Mussolini, Lenin, Stalin or Hitler. He did a wonderful job in unifying China and despite being a communist, he ruled China in a benevolent way, but became increasingly dictatorial. He died in 1976.

Our prime minister at the time, Rob Muldoon, had in that year been the first New Zealand leader to visit communist China, and New Zealand was earlier among the first Western countries to recognise China. The delegation selected included the New Zealand Academy of Fine Arts, which included me — but no women were included, so I went on without Patricia.

China was very interesting in that Mao had been gone only for a short while and the country was just beginning to open up, but culturally there were cracks, particularly in music and education.

The Chinese smoked all the time and we were presented with cigarettes during our visits. The only shops other than the communist-controlled stores were the tobacconists. On one occasion we visited one of these shops, and were almost crowded out by the locals because one of our party had a full beard — nobody had seen one before!

I could not help being impressed by the communist way of life. The children were always beautifully dressed, and they were also well educated. We attended an English class and were impressed with their grasp of the language. Some of the children spoke to us in quite good English.

We were taken round the country, which is very beautiful. Chou En-lai was unlike Mao. He was culturally sophisticated and saved nearly all the wonderful collections of Chinese art from Mao's cleansing. We saw the amazing art collections going back for thousands of years, including the famous jade kings and the figures representing the soldiers of the First Emperor, who reigned in about 500 AD. It had been the custom in the past to bury those troops when the Emperor died.

X

Sketches of politics and social life 1940s–1980s

In the old days the social life in Wellington was very much focused around Government House and we all used to go to parties there. I often wonder whether we were right to abolish knighthoods as nothing really has replaced them. The Order of New Zealand means nothing to people outside New Zealand.

Thanks to having a nanny, Patricia was able to join in a lot of activities. She was local president of the Plunket Society. Walter Nash, our member of parliament, organised cars for the Plunket nurses to travel around in so they could do their work with young mothers and babies in the community. Patricia was also the foundation president of the Wellington Housewives Association. Some of our local friends were antagonistic to the number of Labour Party friends we had, which included Walter Nash, a neighbour as well as local MP, and Percy Dowse, the Hutt Valley mayor, who came from Bethnal Green.

We were also friendly with Sid Holland and his wife. Sid was an old-fashioned democrat. When we visited him he would sit in his braces and collarless shirt and say he liked to feel relaxed. He also liked my wife's bread and had one of our geese for Christmas. He was a wonderful public speaker and was at his best with an unruly crowd. He would persuade noisy speakers to come forward and then deal with them in the nicest way. He was just the man to put National into power after Fraser's oppressive socialist government.

Walter Nash (prime minister 1957–60)

Walter Nash succeeded Holyoake as prime minister in 1957. He was a dedicated socialist who openly stated that he did not think anyone should earn more than £500 per annum. He proceeded to try and introduce socialism into New Zealand. It was not very far from communism.

I knew Walter Nash very well as his family were neighbours of ours in Woburn Road when we lived in Lower Hutt. The government of the time did not provide him with a car, so I used to drive him into town and got to know him very well. He was a sort of Jekyll and Hyde person. He was a wonderful local member and went to great lengths to assist his constituents.

Walter's wife and family were not socialists. His son was a doctor and member of the National Party. Walter used to talk a great deal about not drinking alcohol. In those days the great event in New Zealand was the annual Plunket Ball. Our Plunket Ball was always held in Lower Hutt and Walter Nash would come along. Patricia used to offer him 'orange juice' which was really a strong whisky, which he drank with great delight! When he retired from politics he became Sir Walter. We used to see him at Government House, which was a very different place to what it is today.

National governments 1949–57 and 1960–72

I was a founder member of the National Party in 1936, and when they came to power under Sid Holland in 1949 the right wing expected that all the government controls would be removed. This was not so and I know the reason why. The supporters outside the farming community all benefited from these restrictions. They set up successful businesses (as we did) and so the business community supported continuation of import controls and other restrictions. The irony of the situation was that the Labour Party were the people who eventually removed the restrictions.

My wife was a member of a small committee concerned about opening hours in pubs and hotels in the 1960s. They approached the government with the request that 6pm closing be abolished. Jack Marshall, the deputy prime minister then, opposed this movement. Due to this restriction, few licensed restaurants existed in New Zealand.

Of course drunken parties often took place in private homes given by the young when parents were overseas! I believe that Marshall thought that freedom to drink out of hours would result in an orgy of alcoholism (which has occurred). It would have been much better if the English system had been adopted where bars and hotels close at 2pm and re-open at 5pm, closing again at 11pm. Public opinion forced the government to give way and it was not long before restaurants opened all over the country, some of very high standard.

Keith Holyoake (prime minister 1957, 1960–70)

Keith Holyoake would often visit us in Woburn Road when he was Minister of Agriculture. No one had ever survived being Minister of Agriculture, but he went on to become prime minister. He was a very shrewd politician. When he was prime minister, I became president of the Chamber of Commerce and also the Softgoods Association, and often led delegations to see the PM. He would always ask me what I thought, which was very flattering. I said to him once, "We would like to hear what you think." He took this quite well! I got back at him by saying, "If you want my advice, I think you make yourself too available." He once tried to persuade me to stand for parliament.

I always admired the way he handled the Vietnam War. He did not believe in 'All the way with LBJ' but did not want to offend the Americans. He sent a medical team to Vietnam in 1964 and some volunteer troops in 1965. I was always against the Vietnam War and thought the Americans should never have been involved. The war ended with the utter humiliation of the United States and the weakening of the standing of Europeans in that part of the world.

Robert Muldoon later appointed Holyoake Governor-General to get rid of him. In my view Holyoake could not deal with the role and was quite unacquainted with the formalities and protocols, and also felt there was too much entertaining.

Save Manapouri campaign

Lake Manapouri was under threat because Comalco needed cheap hydroelectric power from the lake for their aluminium processing plant in New Zealand. I believe the whole concept of the Comalco scheme was wrong. Comalco would mine the bauxite and send it down to New Zealand for processing — it was then sent back to Australia. The only reason they did this was because of the very cheap power in New Zealand.

Legislation passed in 1960 allowed the level of Lake Manapouri to be raised by 28 feet to generate an extra 200 megawatts of electricity. This would result in devastation of the lake and surrounding areas. The whole country became alarmed over this issue when the impact of the legislation became evident. In October 1969 several committees formed all over New Zealand to petition the National government. I became involved in Wellington. We got nowhere. We then made an approach to Norman Kirk, who had become leader of the Labour Party. One of the members of my committee in Wellington was an expert in constitutional affairs. His advice to me was that if we presented a petition to parliament it had to first be placed before the House, which took time. We took our petition down and presented it to parliament and they turned us down. We presented another petition, and we continued doing this for some time — and then there was an election in 1972.

I was taken up by plane to see the area. It was pointed out to me what would happen if the lake was raised, which had already occurred at Lake Monowai, a small lake nearby. Undoubtedly all the trees around the lake would die, all the beaches would disappear and the entire area would be spoilt. Kirk was very interested in our submission and agreed to have a look for himself. He came back and told us that he was 100% behind the petition to save the lake.

One of the first things Norman Kirk did when he came to power was to modify the Manapouri scheme to remove the threat to the lake.

Some time later I expressed an interest to visit the Comalco plant in Australia. Their reaction was "Oh no, we can't have that man visiting the plant!" What they had forgotten was that we were supplying their canteens with our goods. I got my firm to ring up and request: "Our chairman would like to come around and look around the plant." On that basis I was welcome to visit! I think the Comalco deal was a very bad one for this country.

We are living in a world at the moment where we are wondering where we are going to get more power. Comalco takes a great deal of the power produced in the South Island. If we had not entered into this wonderful agreement, there would have been plenty of power for everybody.

The following is a letter I wrote to Les Hutchins in June 2002.

"I do not imagine that you would believe that I am approaching 96 and still fit and well.

"I am sure that most people in the North Island had no idea what was going on in the Manapouri crisis at the time. I certainly did not. I was having lunch in the Wellington Club when I noticed a meeting being held which Ian Prior was chairing. I was very surprised to see Dr Sutch there and went over to see what was going on. I found out very quickly. It was the opening meeting of the Save Manapouri campaign in the Wellington area. Nominations were being called for the position of chairman, and all those present began to give reasons why they could not take the post — mainly because they were connected with the government in some way or another. Finally, they turned to me, and as I couldn't think of any excuse, I found myself in the chair. I will never regret what was a wonderful experience for me.

"A short while ago, Ian Prior sent me a copy of your book *Making Waves* which I have read with great interest. I had not realised the extent to which the campaign was instigated and motivated by you almost on your own. Without your efforts, the lake would never have been saved. The book is the story of your remarkable development from a very small beginning. I cannot understand why the main part of the campaign is so rarely mentioned in your book.

"The committee, of which I was chairman, worked very hard. We met once a week. Unfortunately I cannot remember the details and lost all records when my house was burnt down a few years ago.

"The committee had the advantage of being in constant touch with most of the people concerned. We raised money by using various devices. I remember well the issue of the 'Manapouri Dollar.' This was a huge success and was responsible for raising a lot

```
╔══════════════════════════════════════╗
║   Save Manapouri Campaign            ║
║              (ASSETS:- NATURAL)      ║
║  50c      ONE SHARE        50c       ║
║  CAPITAL: 30,000 Ordinary Shares @ 50c        PERPETUAL DIVIDEND : Retention
║  SHAREHOLDERS: New Zealand Public   N° 8151   of Lake Manapouri in its natural state
║         Dated this 1st day of June, 1970    David G. Kember, Secretary.
║   This Certificate acknowledges your donation to the National Save Manapouri Campaign
╚══════════════════════════════════════╝
```

of the money that enabled us to pay for a great deal of advertising, as well as a lot of the other expenses. None of our members were paid anything: in fact, one of our members was part-Maori and helped us to get Maori support as well.

"One of our members was a lawyer and told us that if we made a submission to parliament, it would have to be presented to the House for consideration. We managed, because of this, to delay a decision being made until after the next election.

"I wonder if you have ever given thought as to what would happen if we had failed. Our next move was to approach Norman Kirk. Together with another member of our committee I met him, and he listened very carefully to what we had to say. He decided to go down and have a look for himself. Without his support I doubt if we would ever have succeeded. I formed a very high opinion of his integrity. I do believe that he was driven to his death by the hard 'right wing.' (I feel that they would do the same to the present prime minister [Helen Clark] if they could!)

"When the Labour Party came into power, they took immediate action and saved the lake for the future.

Recalling the Manapouri Campaign: David Kember, Jack Harris and Ian Prior at the Wellington Club, 1994.

"I read that the whole scheme has been a great success and that the river is now navigable: the fishing has improved and Comalco has enough water for its needs. I tried at that time to have a look at the Comalco plant for myself. I was refused entry until they discovered that I was from Bing Harris who was the main supplier for their canteen. I was then given VIP treatment!

"I am very fond of oysters. I have been informed that at that time the effluent from the smelter had polluted the beds. Now oysters are available, but unfortunately in Wellington they are very expensive!"

The 1984 Labour government

When the Lange/Roger Douglas (Labour) government came into power in 1984, it was Roger Douglas who brought down the socialist edifice.

I knew Roger Douglas very well. He used to copy all his speeches for me for comment. I said to him one day, "Do you know what is holding the farming community back? Death duties. Every time farmers have to pay death duties, they have to sell their stock and deplete their farms." Death duties were soon abolished — that is something I helped to achieve for New Zealand.

Lange was a brilliant speaker but, in my opinion, was too immature to hold the office of prime minister — he was in his early 40s then.

Distinguished visitors from Europe

The Crown Prince of Sweden was a special visitor to our home. He was a charming guest and easy to entertain. It was a lovely day and we went for a walk in the garden. We had locked up our two Dalmatian dogs (rather brainless animals) but he fell on them with great interest. He told us that his father as a boy used to be taken to Windsor Park by Queen Victoria. On one side of the carriage ran two Dalmatians (carriage dogs), hence his interest in our two.

Among our distinguished visitors in the 1970s was Willi Brandt, the former Chancellor of Germany. He arrived with an escort of security men who remained in our driveway entrance during his visit.

Some of our distinguished visitors had little to discuss with the government, and Brandt was one of these. He had evidently heard of New Zealand as the most beautiful group of islands in the world. He spoke perfect English and was good company and easy to talk to.

I read his book not so long ago and I am taking this opportunity to comment on it. Willi Brandt is a convinced conservationist and no doubt his visit was also to speak to like minds here. On one or two points I disagree with him, probably because it is some years since he wrote the book. Population growth is now slowing down and most western countries are warned about the problems connected with a falling birthrate. Knowledge of this will continue to grow and will create other problems connected with old age. He also refers to the possible annihilation of the human race, which has always seemed to be very likely.

Thinking things over, I do not believe that this will occur. When gunpowder was first invented it became a weapon that destroyed millions of people, but they still managed to increase in numbers. Since the shield was invented to protect man against the sword, other means of protection have been developed as different dangers presented themselves.

I have no doubt that, apart from the loss of millions of lives, a similar development will occur and protection can also be developed against the bomb. Selected humans will find protection deep underground and some humans will survive on earth.

Disease is just as dangerous. Medical science is developing to protect us against cancer and Aids and will continue to find cures for diseases that threaten mankind.

XI

Te Rama, Waikanae

After the war we did not go overseas. I bought a beach cottage at Waikanae. At that time there was nothing at the beach except for a post office and a general store. The village had only a small newsagent on the corner by the railway station. It belonged to a German refugee. I bought a little pug dog and went down to the newsagent, who greeted me with: "Kleines Möpschen!" I asked him what 'Möpschen' was. "It's a little dog." So, all my dogs subsequently were named 'Mops'.

I was getting a bit fed up with having to go to the beach house — but it was fun for the children. We had our home in Woburn, Lower Hutt, which we had had built for us in the 1930s and spent the weekends at the beach cottage.

One day in 1952, quite by chance, we noticed the homestead on State Highway One was up for sale. I had always been curious about this place, so up we went and had a look. There was the old house looking very dilapidated, and sixteen hectares of land that went with the property. It was situated up on the hill to the right of the highway, just south of the Waikanae railway bridge.

I did not really think seriously about buying this huge house with the land and bush on it. I put in a bid for £10,000 and thought no more about it until the land agent rang me and told me I had bought it! So, we had three houses: one in Woburn, the

Te Rama, drawing printed on a Christmas greetings card from the Harrises, about 1959.

beach cottage at Waikanae and the homestead. We couldn't keep them all so the first thing I did was to get rid of the beach cottage, which was not that difficult.

We bought the house in 1952 — it had not been occupied for some time and was in a terrible state. The extraordinary thing was that it had not burnt down a long time ago. After we had bought it the first thing I discovered was that all the drainage was running into a pool of muck underneath the house. The next thing I discovered was that the electrical wiring was all faulty, so I had the house rewired.

A curious thing about the house was that it was insulated with flax, which was packed thoroughly into the walls and provided very good insulation. The water supply was brought down from an intake up in the top of the hills and I replaced that with a bore with gave us excellent water.

When I bought the place, the people who owned it before me

called it 'The Hill'. I had a close friend, Mick Pomare, who came up to visit us. I asked him what its real name was. His reply was 'Te Rama.' I discovered when visiting Malaya that 'rama' was a Malay word too. It means 'gleam of light.' So, Te Rama it was.

The house was alive with rats and mice when we moved in: it was really awful. To deal with the rats I got some cats, which unfortunately reduced the bird population. We would have had almost every native bird in the bush there. It was a lovely place to be. The property was full of the most wonderful birds — all sorts of native birds, even kiwis living in the bush behind the house. I didn't know at the time what a kiwi's call was, but I knew Sir Charles Fleming, the great bird man, very well. He used to come up and listen to the birds. We had every native tree you could imagine up there including nikau palms and tree ferns. Then the possums came and the trouble started.

As time went on the house became too big for us, as all our children had by this time left home. Also the cost of maintenance was high and was getting to be a bit of a strain, which was something I had not realised when I bought the place.

At the time Te Rama burnt down I was due to re-roof and re-paint as part of ongoing maintenance on the building. We had a married couple, Joan and Brian Hathaway, living in the cottage on the property and employed to keep an eye on things and help with routine maintenance work. It was they who had to deal with the fire while we were away on holiday.

An account of the fire written by Joan Hathaway

"Wednesday 10 July 1996 is implanted forever in our lives, but the morning was like any other. How were we to know our lives were to be traumatised later?

"I had decided to make a start on the big house's cleaning as

Sir Jack and Lady Harris were away. I went over at 8.30am and worked until 4pm, really getting into it. I polished, washed and cleaned my way to the kitchen. I finished by cleaning out Papeeto's cage — he was full of beans, bouncing around his cage. I was too tired to carry him over to the cottage, so decided I would get him the next day, although he was quite happy. I left the radio on for company for him. Poor bird — his time was running out.

"4.45pm — I went back over and fed the two cats, had one more look around as we always kept the place locked up. Everything looked lovely, the floors, silver, old china were gleaming. I did not know this would be my last look at all the beautiful things in the historic homestead built in the early 1900s.

"Around 6.30pm I was just dishing out our evening meal at the cottage where Brian and I had lived for 12 years.

"The lights flickered then went out, plunging us into darkness (no street lights). Brian rang the power board to see what was wrong, meanwhile I had gone around to the kitchen to light candles so we could have our meal. This is when I noticed what looked like someone flashing an orange torch on the back porch. We both went out to investigate and could hear a popping noise. When we got over the main house the switchboard was ablaze. Brian grabbed an extinguisher that was kept on the porch, but it made no impression.

"I ran to the cottage and dialled 111: it was now about 7.05pm. I told the operator it was urgent, being an old house, and to please hurry: I said I would wait at the bottom of the drive to guide the fire brigade up. It seemed like hours before one engine came from the Paraparaumu Fire Station. They got stuck on the bend and when I rounded the top of the drive my heart sank, the roof was well alight.

"Brian had gone inside but the thick black smoke overcame him and a fireman helped him out. The dry wood, the walls stuffed with flax, just took off. The water situation was desperate — the reservoir ran out and the swimming pool was emptied by now. We had five fire engines and 30 firefighters working on the blaze: they were bringing water up. It was a horrible sight and we felt so helpless.

"One of the firefighters fell through the staircase and the rescue helicopter was called. Beacons were placed in the centre paddock. Remembering how dark it was, the pilot did a great job landing.

"Two other firefighters were overcome by the heat and smoke. Water was sprayed on the big tree to save the cottage. The wine cellar went up, exploding like World War II. The fire chief brought in some spotlights to help them see. Just one corner of the beautiful house remained; we were devastated and so felt so bereft for the Harrises. Everything gone, a lifetime of memories gone. Paintings, furniture, china, silver — nothing spared and poor Papeeto — what an end.

"It was around 2.30am when they started to pull out. When the blazing lights were turned off, it all seemed like a nightmare. We retreated to the cottage, no lights or heat to warm us. We sat totally stunned and shocked, unable to comprehend the total devastation fire can do.

"Dawn brought the ghastly sight even more clearly to view. It was so sad — Te Rama was gone."

Leaving Te Rama

The fire razed the house, except for one corner — it was a complete ruin. A great many trees were also burnt, which was very sad. The beautiful bush was untouched. We had to decide what we would do, whether to re-build or sell.

We sold the land to people called Fisher. Instead of rebuilding the old house they renovated the cottage, which was previously occupied by the Hathaways. With the help of an architect they turned it into a beautiful little house. It became their weekend family home. It was intriguing to see the transformation.

I had covenanted all the bush and a large area of land around the house to the Queen Elizabeth II Trust, which I am pleased about.

A little bit of history

On the hill overlooking the river you could see indentations. During tribal wars a lookout was kept on the hill to watch out for Te Rauparaha and his activities. They used to light a bonfire across from this river and when they saw canoes coming across from Kapiti Island to 'collect dinner' they could be forewarned of Te Rauparaha's arrival. I made some enquiries about this. What used to happen was that as soon as they saw the island dwellers approaching they scuttled up to Kapakapanui, which means 'place of the copper pots.' They used to have their little feasts up in the hills!

My nephew Jack Penman is of Maori descent. His family came from the Wairarapa and is also descended from Te Rauparaha.

I learnt a lot about the Maori here. In the early days there was bush all around this area. They cleared most of the land to feed sheep and cattle. The original Europeans who settled there built a house in Waikanae, which overlooked the Maori chief's house there. The chief took his tribe around and burnt their house down because he would not have a European overlooking his pa. The family who bought Te Rama left the bush intact so that the Maori down in the village couldn't see the house, otherwise the homestead would have been burnt down too. So, the bush was left as a safety net around the property preventing it from destruction until the unfortunate fire in 1996.

Waimahoe was the original homestead built in 1894 on the Te Rama site, but sadly it was burnt down in 1903, nine years after it was built. It was rebuilt, its original name disappeared, and the new home named Te Rama when we came to live in it in 1952. It is interesting and most unusual that there were two fires on this site, completely destroying the two houses.

Te Rama after the fire, 1996.

XII

Patricia's story of Te Rama

Te Rama — a most desirable site

We had had a peculiarly difficult weekend. The weather had been undecided about rain but it had known all about wind. The family had been forced to huddle in a small seaside cottage at Waikanae Beach which was in no way suitable for close communication between two adults, three children, two dogs and the family cats. None of the party had enjoyed the resultant conflicts.

The grown-ups had been plagued by all the irritations which can be inflicted by bored children. The cats had been prevented from hunting and one of them had been sick in my underclothes. The dogs had been restless and had asked to be let out of the door far more often than necessary. Above all, the sand had blown over the food and across the floor. Somehow it had even managed to penetrate our teeth and ears.

In short — we had *had* weekends at the beach.

The drive back to the city was a silent one for the first few miles, then, rather to break the ominous silence than with any serious intent, I said that I had noticed that there was an old house for sale in the valley, above the river. I had caught sight of a sign on a gatepost, which merely stated that "this desirable site with

Patricia with dogs at Te Rama.

homestead and amenities" was to be auctioned together with forty acres of native bush and pasture. No mention was made of the price or of the condition of this high-sounding estate.

My husband digested this information for a few minutes, then, when I had almost forgotten my conversational gambit, came back at me with the quiet statement that he was "fed up with the beach, sick of spending Friday afternoon packing the car to go away, and Sunday evening cleaning up and re-packing children, animals, and left-over food into the same car in order to make the return trip." He had enough self-control and tact not to cast aspersions on Ginger Nut and his colleague (cats), or on Schnapps the poodle and Mops the pug. That would have been more than my state of nervous tension and exhaustion could have survived.

Not being notable for patience, or for too much looking before leaping, I at once proceeded to find the man who was advertised as the agent for the property. He was an old friend (which was perhaps fortunate) but he was also an estate agent. This dual capacity meant that while he was convinced that we had gone mad, he was ready to encourage our fantasy.

Two days later we were escorted on a visit to view the old house and to be shown its hidden charms. These were well concealed! The place was enormous and sprawled across an overgrown garden. The native bush was indeed lovely but had encroached on the whole establishment that one felt near to suffocation by its green embrace. The old homestead looked like a cross between a railway station and a rundown preparatory school — a simile made more apt by the colour scheme of the paintwork which was an elegant combination of tired yellow on wooden walls and brick red on the peeling iron roof. There was also a shed and a gardener's loo dominating the stony courtyard where we parked our car.

Inside, the rooms were huge and high. The dining room had a fully gabled ceiling which gave it a dismal resemblance to a school chapel. There was a long, narrow central corridor which looked and felt like a railway tunnel. This dark crevasse was further embellished by an extraordinary heating stove which thrust a black chimney up through two stories to the roof and thence into the sky. This sinister phallic symbol was ice cold to the touch and so was I.

There were numerous outbuildings whose use was mysterious to us. One appeared to have started life as a Victorian gazebo but had now become the residence of a vast collection of spiders and a few rats and mice. The spiders in this part of the country will, I have since discovered, invade any room or building round the place. Unless drastic measures are taken every day, they will busy themselves by making a very good imitation of Miss Havisham's wedding feast.

It didn't really seem that we were going to be encouraged to uproot ourselves and our family in order to enjoy the pleasures of a country home.

Together with the ever-hopeful, though increasingly tepid, agent, we continued our tour of inspection. The garden had glorious old trees and some well-grown shrubs. There was an asparagus bed, which was about to yield. A stream ran down from the hills and we were assured that we would always have an ample water supply of our own. There was plenty of room for Margaret to keep a pony. There was a dilapidated tennis court, huge stables, a loft and hen house and a kitchen that could be made into the heart of the house (with a lot of imagination).

In fact, the thing which broke down our resistance had nothing to do with these features. It was the fact that we would be sheltered from the beastly wind that broke itself here on the hill behind the house. Lack of the maddening wind, and the birds which suddenly decided that we must know best, as well as the worst, and broke into full song. A tui called to his friends. A bellbird hit his top note while grey warblers joined in the chorus. As a final gesture, several wood pigeons rested on the branch of a dead tree and eyed us in a manner which we chose to imagine was not unfriendly.

We fell for their charms and decided, rather rashly, to 'make an offer.' This in simple English means that Party A suggests a price which he thinks he can afford. This is immediately spurned by the agent as unrealistic. Party B (the vendor) then makes his suggestion. This is turned down as "inflated" and "out of the question." The agent mutters about clients who are unreasonable and produces a compromise bid. (I have a suspicion that this is the price that he had intended to obtain at the start.) Almost accidentally — you have bought a house!

The catch about this is that we already had a large and very attractive home in the city and a cottage on the beach as well. No wonder the agent rejoiced. He had three deals in the bag instead of one: while we, poor innocents, had three houses on our hands!

The latest acquisition being old, a bit dilapidated, without most of the necessary conveniences, in urgent need of redecoration, cold, damp, depressing and overgrown by herbaceous intruders. In our saner moments we were perfectly aware that it was not the kind of place that any sensible, conventional citizen would contemplate, if given time to think. We didn't (think, I mean). We were far too besotted by the contrast between our new purchase and the rather unattractive suburban city environment, which was all that we had been able to find since our arrival in New Zealand.

At this stage of the proceedings, there was a lull while papers were signed and bank managers placated. We did have sufficient cunning to decide that, in the meanwhile, we would only use the place as a holiday home and would sell the beach cottage. This was just as well, because the new acquisition was more than thirty miles from my husband's office and would obviously need careful examination before we could embark on major alterations. We also had to consider the family and allow them to become accustomed to the idea of being uprooted from the quasi-suburbs and pitchforked into what looked suspiciously like a hillbilly way of life.

On top of these considerations, we had also to pay attention to our mixed bag of pets. In fact, we had to make up our minds if this was the way we wanted to live for most of our future. It could be no hasty or ill-conceived decision.

The younger children presented no problems. Margaret was mad about horses anyway, while the youngest of the trio was perfectly happy to spend his holidays catching eels in the stream or making a house in the branches of the huge tree that dominated the courtyard. The eldest was more difficult to placate, as he was old enough to have put down roots in his present environment and was no countryman in any case. I think he only softened when he discovered that he could shoot as many possums as he could find and that he would be congratulated for his prowess as the beasts were living happily on the orchard fruit.

The dogs didn't mind so long as they were in our company. The cats were overjoyed to become working cats as the house was alive with bush rats who ran across the attic all night and who chewed the buttons off our clothes! The cats, quite correctly, felt that they were the most essential members of the household.

The kitchen arrangements were obscure to a degree, which left me completely puzzled for a long time, until in fact I began to reorganise them.

There was a large central room that contained an electric stove, circa 1920, one table, one chair, a calendar for 1929, and an alcove which housed the wood-fired boiler from which we had to draw our hot water supply. From this area there were two doors, one of which led to a scullery, which was equipped with a tub and a cold-water tap and another, which opened into a sort of butler's pantry, which had a sink and draining board. There was a further door into a walk-in pantry which was inhabited by huge rats and tiny mice. There were also two cupboard-like rooms off the scullery that had once housed the housemaid and a tweeny (I think). The result of this arrangement, of what is usually referred to as the 'domestic offices' was that, in order to produce the simplest meal, it was necessary to walk from pantry to stove, from stove to scullery, from scullery to table and from table to sink, about a million times.

The boiler enjoyed a malicious sense of humour and always managed to go out half an hour before I wanted a bath — and I mean wanted in the fullest sense. It would refuse to be coaxed back to life until long after we were all covered with soot and far too tired to summon enough energy to light so much as a match. Our first improvement would have to be in the hot water service if were to live in the most modest comfort.

It was two years before we could make up our minds that, whatever the disadvantages, we wanted to make our permanent home here in the bush. We had by then grown accustomed to listening for the birds in the early mornings.

We wanted to raise our own poultry and fatten our own turkey for Christmas dinner. There was by now a stout pony in the stable, where the cats had established a hunting routine. Even the garden had begun to yield unsuspected treasures, once we had learned to find our way among the weeds and undergrowth. I had a whole bed of violets in bloom and the big magnolia was covered with buds.

The change would be tremendous, but, we told ourselves and anyone else who would listen, it would be a better life for all of us once we had turned the old house into something more suitable to our conception of a country home.

The major step forward was when we at last consulted an architect. Then we knew that we were on our way, whatever the results might be. Fortunately for us, our man was endowed with a sense of humour, considerable experience, and a most unusual willingness to try anything, so long as the scheme could be made to conform to local body rules and structural possibility. He was a gem as far as we were concerned, as we had already suffered from the peculiarities of the New Zealand attitude to life. They are the most delightful people on earth so long as you don't want to break away from their pattern. If you are unwilling to conform to this accepted plan you must resign yourself to a long campaign of frustration.

"It can't be done."

"Why not?"

"Well … it hasn't been done before."

"Well, why hasn't it been done before?"

This last question brings forth so many answers that they can only be returned by submitting a multitude of forms (in quintuplicate) to suitable government officials, and then waiting for their answers, which are usually contradictory. This is a country where sheep and civil servants proliferate. The only difference being that the sheep give a good return in the shape of wool and meat for their keep, or at least they did then.

The counter-move to all this bureaucracy is the phrase: "We'll give it a go." This expression is the foundation of survival in New Zealand. It can be translated to mean that one is willing to try and breach almost impregnable fortresses that have been erected by officialdom in order to prevent anyone doing what they want to do. It needs all the determination and cunning of a guerrilla army to carry out a simple plan in the face of such blanketing discouragement: but there is a considerable amount of pleasure to be gained from defeating the enemy, and that is perhaps why so many otherwise placid citizens will suddenly decide to "give it a go" and rout the forces of convention by the sheer unexpectedness of their attack.

There didn't appear to be any proper name attached to the

homestead when we bought it. It had been carved off a much larger sheep farm and no one had re-christened it. We asked a Maori friend of ours to suggest a suitable name and he promptly gave us the assurance that it would be perfectly easy for him to find out the original title as it had once formed part of his family's estate. After some discussion and consultation, he told us that it had been known as 'Te Rama' which could be translated to mean 'The Torch light' or the 'light on the hill.' In fact, it was a way of saying that there had been a settlement there in the old days and that the hill had been used as a lookout and a fort. We have since found traces of this fortification on the top of the ridge overlooking the sea.

So! Te Rama it was to us. We began to feel like pioneers and to identify ourselves with our grandparents who had left the Old World to make their way in the distant colonies. Mine were, in fact, my great-great-grandparents who had come to Australia at a very early stage in its career.

This decision to try to make our domestic life in a more rural atmosphere than we were previously used to was not a new dream come true. I had for many years been sure that if we were going to stay in New Zealand, the so-called city was not for me. I wasn't too sure about Jack. He had never lived for any length of time in the country since having spent his holidays on a farm in England during World War I. He had been at Cambridge, then in Paris, Hamburg and Berlin before he decided to go to the southern hemisphere to see for himself what was happening to a family business which had been established in Dunedin by his grandfather.

Jack had found himself fascinated by the ways of commerce and, much to his astonishment, chairman, in his twenty-seventh year, of a company which had been scorned by his father and most of the rest of the owners, who were firmly convinced that civilisation stopped short at the end of State Highway One. I rather suspect

Patricia's story of Te Rama

Patricia, 1960s.

it was the women of the family who disliked the idea of living so far away. But the result had been that their heritage in New Zealand was regarded as slightly indelicate. I didn't have any idea if either of us would be any good at country life, but I had become sufficiently acclimatised to be prepared to "give it a go", and to my delight, so was Jack. We were, after all, the parents of three New Zealanders by this time.

It had been impossible to implement my plans before the lucky day when we caught sight of that *For Sale* notice on the gate. First of all there were babies, then the long years of the war, then small children at day schools. We had petrol rationing to make it out of the question for Jack to commute every day over a distance of more than thirty miles. Most people thought that we were mad anyway and pointed out that no one lived in the country unless they were economically dependent on farming. The discovery of Te Rama came at exactly the right moment for us. I wasn't going to be discouraged.

The most significant thing to remember when embarking upon the restoration of an old house is that it will cost considerably more than twice as much as you could possibly imagine any building operation could do. Don't fool yourself, it WILL!

The plumbing, which runs to every room, will turn out to have the most complete collection of leaks that you could wish to see — even if you are a plumber's mate.

The electric power is connected through the entire place — but the wires are so tangled and so exposed by the teeth of rats, that the only safe course (says the man from the Power Board) is to start again with completely new and well insulated wiring. It doesn't matter to him that it will be about as costly as wiring the Albert Hall. After all, no one in his senses builds a house of this size at modern prices, unless they happen to be in the building trade!

In spite of all this, it was fun when each little piece was broken away and partitions removed and the light began to pour through the big windows. When the numerous box-like rooms at the back were thrown into each other to give a more spacious interior, we started to see what we were doing. Then, at last, we were sure that this was to be our true home.

The full gable in the dining room was one of our worst trials. We had to decide whether to disguise it, obliterate it completely or to be bold and feature it as a talking point in our décor. After much discussion we made up our minds that if one has an architectural oddity, the best thing to do is to draw attention to it. This wasn't difficult, as if it were to survive, it couldn't be ignored. So, we painted the whole affair rose pink!! As I had found some old Toile de Jouy wallpaper depicting a suitable rustic scene in eighteenth century France, and some delightful Hepplewhite chairs, we were able to produce a most satisfactory Provençal room.

We had to move a few doors and a wall in the process, but the effect was delicious and fully merited the gilt chandelier by the Adams Brothers which I found later in London and which, weighing as much as a small railway engine, was finally hung by chains from the beam at the apex of the ceiling. There it still hangs as though it had been designed for just that particular place and it only sways very gently in an earthquake, which is fortunate, because if it ever fell, it could bring most of the roof and the attics with it.

The hall had to be opened so that we could enter the house from the courtyard, thus bypassing the exceedingly narrow front verandah and the existing front door, which had stained glass squares and a large bell (no wires attached). By sacrificing a 'servant's' room, we made a most charming archway between the new front door and the hall (whose full horror had been eliminated by now). This meant that we could see right through the house to the outdoor living area, which was to be our summer assembly place for months of every year.

I forgot to mention that the telephone jutted out from the wall of the old hall in the most sinister way, as it was the first object to emerge when one's eyes adjusted themselves to the gloom of the cavernous passageway. All that one wanted to say was inhibited by the Gothic atmosphere and by the fact that we were on a 'party line.' This meant that the whole village were regaled by snatches of our conversation which had been overheard by other parties on the line. This didn't worry the grown-ups particularly, but it was very annoying to a teenager who was in a perpetual state of courtship.

The other unregretted casualty of the reconstruction had been the little house in the courtyard. We had no wish to retain a 'dunny' immediately outside the entrance! At that stage we didn't have a gardener and it was both hideous and rotten with borer. Out it went on our colossal bonfire. This rubbish fire was the fate for a collection of miscellaneous arisings. Old furniture, broken bedsteads, a collection of newspapers dating from the Boer War, I should imagine, a box full of ancient schoolbooks and a pile of long-forgotten accounts. We found a fiery end for some of our own hoard of useless possessions too. We could at least move into the new house without bringing with us anything that we could manage to discard.

While the phoenix was arising, we were trying to winkle ourselves out of our city home and were thus able to be ruthless with the accumulation of articles which had been carefully stored in the pious hope that "they might be useful some day." We also had to find a buyer for the house we were leaving, and here we came into contact with the realities of 'Real' estate.

Possibly one of the most misleading facts of life is that the deal with house or land (or anything else that one wants to sell) is an entirely different kettle of fish to the deal where one is considered likely to buy. The two transactions have no point of resemblance whatsoever. Don't let yourself be taken in by the fact that the agent says he has a fine waiting list of clients.

Prospective buyers came in driblets. The house had to be waiting for their inspection. Tidy. Unnaturally well groomed. The toys in the right boxes and the cupboards neatly arranged.

No wonder we had so much fodder for the bonfire!

The people who walked through the house with the agent, or alone, were probably nice characters with charming manners, except when they were looking over a house that someone else wanted to sell. They now became cautious and wanted to find faults. Women who had never known more than a 'dining alcove' complained that the distance from the dining room to the stove was too great and that the food would be cold on arrival at table and refused to notice that there were very efficient heated serving arrangements. Men who had cheerfully mowed a tiny lawn on Sunday mornings asked why there was no swimming pool. The double garage was too small for three cars. A whole new range of domestic objections came to light and we began to feel positively apologetic for a house which had always been admired by our more sophisticated friends. What is more, reasonable men showed themselves quite incapable of making decisions or of telling the truth about their plans.

One member of the Corps Diplomatique, having inspected the premises several times, would give no clear 'yes' or 'no' to the proposition. But he had invitations printed for a reception of that address in four weeks' time. It was a revealing experience of human behaviour at its least attractive.

While all this chattering was taking place, I was doing my best to make the architect, builder, plumber, electrician and the hordes of other men who crawled about the semi-restored building (looking a trifle surprised), understand that we had every intention of spending Christmas in the house, come hell or high water. They did their best to finish the job but were hampered by all kinds of infuriating delays. The joinery wasn't finished, the wallpaper hadn't arrived from France, the painter was ill. All the crop of frustrations which can flourish during building operations were there to harass us, and the weather joined in the fun. It rained and rained and rained. New pipes overflowed onto new paintwork. The septic tank was flooded. Hydrangea the hen was washed downstream with her chickens. It was a nightmare of mud and mildew, and almost turned me from my purpose — but not quite.

In the end, towards the middle of December, we announced that we intended to move in, no matter what the conditions. We had at last sold the other house and our furniture had to be evacuated. The children were coming home from boarding school for the summer vacation and we would all be homeless unless we had somewhere habitable to shelter us.

Loads of furniture and personal belongings were deposited in half-completed rooms while the removal van carried out a shuttle service from house to house. The animals in their baskets, cages, and aquaria were installed in the most suitable places (for them not for us). We fell over them every time we tried to arrange our own belongings. On the actual moving-in day there was a cloudburst and seven inches of rain fell on us: there were also five workmen in the hall and they informed us that we couldn't walk down it as they were applying the polish to its tiles. The stove fused and the thermostat on the new hot water service was set so high that we only just escaped scalding ourselves!

Even our stalwart Nanny, who had stuck bravely by us in silent disapproval, looked like caving in under the strain. But at last, we were *in*. After considerable detective work we found a bottle of something or other and toasted ourselves and Te Rama out of jelly glasses, as the china had been put in an inaccessible spot. We dined in our rather formal gabled room, but our meal consisted of sausages grilled on the open fire which had been lit to reduce the dampness, but which was now our only cooking place. It would have been easier to do the grilling if we had not tripped over the cats and dogs that were firmly determined to retain the best places in its warmth. At last, we managed to make up enough beds to give us our desperately needed rest.

The first night in occupation was punctuated by alarms. The youngest of the family woke up screaming and didn't know where he was. While Nanny coped with him my black cat arrived at our bedside with an enormous rat which he proceeded to play with around the room. The night trains whistled and panted as they passed the gate below. An owl hooted at regular intervals outside our window. The old house creaked and groaned in the wind as though it wished to complain at its transformation. We all slept in snatches of exhausted unconsciousness.

Morning brought an improvement all round. We managed to find many necessities which had seemed to us to be lost forever. Familiar toys lay about on the carpets and we began to shake down into some sort of routine. The two older children were arriving home in the afternoon and I had to set about preparing the 'First Night Home Dinner' which was part of our family ritual.

At last it had stopped raining for a while and I was able to find flowers to arrange in the rooms: this was a real piece of settling in as I have an obsession about a house which is not full of the colour and scent of flowers — to me it lacks life and is depressingly un-lived in. So, there were bouquets on every table or shelf which held a vase.

Our workmen also deserted us for a short period and it was possible to use the lavatories without seeing a cheerful face grinning over the top of the windows! This habit had proved most disconcerting to all of us, and Nanny positively bridled at such intrusion of our privacy.

The new kitchen was unalloyed joy to work in: we had removed partitions between the various segments and now the scullery was a modern laundry (and always referred to as the 'cat's kitchen') while the old walk-in cupboard had been transformed into a bar with shelves full of gleaming glasses, and our stocks of liquor ranged in racks under the counter. This counter opens into the dining room and can be shut off if necessary by a rolling shutter.

Above the new sink and the dishwashing machine there is now a wide picture window through which the garden can be seen as one does the chores. This window was one of our architect's major achievements as it replaced the alcove in which the malicious boiler had puffed or, more aptly, faded away. The main difficulty in doing this had been caused by the necessity to take down the tall chimney, which had soared above the alcove.

There were six of these chimneys round the house: they had been made from handmade bricks salvaged from a much earlier house that had been burned down at the end of the 19th century. They are some of the tallest chimneys in this country: all our friends had eyed them with misgiving and had muttered that they "wouldn't like to be under one of those in an earthquake." It was reassuring to find that, in order to pull down the unwanted one, we had to use a bulldozer and, even then, the chimney resisted to the end. They have been constructed to withstand the hardest strain, and the lovely old bricks are only a veneer over some kind of iron hard flues, which are almost impossible to crack. It was reassuring to know this; but our newly planted shrubs were not improved by the intrusion of a bulldozer round the side of the house.

This kitchen, with its gay flowered wallpaper and its pale blue floor and bench tops, was to become the social centre of the establishment: I have counted as many as fifteen adults and five children, all with glasses in their hands, all talking at once, standing round, while I cooked dinner. It attracts all our visitors and is truly what is described in America as a conversation area.

Most of the conversations held here are stimulating, some are sad, some most intense, but all are fascinating in their unlikely subject matter. Love affairs, matrimonial troubles, family feuds, business propositions, illness, success, failure — all have been at some time aired in this place.

When at last the family was complete and we had assembled round the table, the usual arguments and discussions of events broke out in full spate, and we knew that we were truly 'at home' at last. My spirits rose in proportion to the way in which the rooms absorbed their occupants and I forgot all about the trials

Te Rama in its heyday.

and tribulations of our transference. When, late that night, I did my last survey of the household, I knew that all was well at Te Rama. There was a cat on the end of each of three beds, a small dog was on one as well, a saddle was carefully balanced on the stair rail and a pair of running shoes, spikes up, had been left on the shiny new floor. The atmosphere of the house was welcoming to the newcomers and one could see that it would, in a few years, be as comfortably shaped to our way of living as a favourite old pair of shoes.

With the years this has happened, and now that the furniture is shabby and a bit knocked about, and the family have all grown up and have their own lives to lead, there is still an ambience which only comes to houses which are loved, and lived in to the full.

Patricia, towards the end of her life.

Time

by Patricia Harris

Time is demolishing me slowly but wantonly,
    as days go by and I remember less.
Was youth and strength so easily passed on to age?
And memories built so frail that they can crumble in a day,
    leaving no trace of youth?
But yet the memories prevail so strong, and still so warm,
    that life depends upon their rich recall, into the present,
    with its needs to face what must be realised today.
And still the memories prevail, so precious and so real to me,
    that I must learn so late in life the strength to recognize,
    the strength of memories' rewards
    and how to take the path that waits.

XIII
Doomsday

I am a very old man, retired for many years now. This has given me the time to think about whether life has any meaning, about our place as humans in the world in which we live, and whether there is any logical explanation for the universe in which our world is an infinitely small part.

Thoughts on this subject by philosophers and the religions have been much distorted by the teachings of men who lived two thousand years ago, a time in history which has little relevance to the world in which we live today. I think that something can be learnt about ethics from the teachings of Jesus. The opinions expressed, including other subjects on a basis of profound ignorance, seem to be grotesque today.

Most young people do not accept the religious teachings of the churches and turn to sport, sex, violence and drugs instead.

I believe that much can be learnt from studying the discoveries of astronomers and scientists in recent years. It seems to me that a definite pattern emerges from their studies, which is consistent throughout the universe.

First of all, there is its size. No one knows exactly how large it is, but we have to consider a universe of millions of light years. There is also the possible existence of other universes.

The majority of astronomers accept the theory of the Big Bang, but the Big Bang cannot have emerged from nothing before it. Perhaps it is merely a part of the circle of birth, growth and death which is a consistent feature of the universe.

I believe in eternity. Many reject this belief because many generations of people accept the concept of a divine creator, but the circle (of which there is no beginning and no end) can express eternity.

Einstein discovered that light and time are bent, in which case, light probably moves in an infinite circle. It has also been discovered that there is no such thing as an absolute vacuum in the universe, although in some areas between constellations cosmic dust must be very thin. There is cosmic dust everywhere and in some areas there are vast clouds of dust.

Out of this dust stars are formed by gravitation, which consolidates the dust. The consolidation by gravitation heats it up to a point at which atomic power is generated and the stars begin to shine. The stars become hotter in time and some of the larger stars become so hot that they consume their own heat and collapse into themselves, forming black holes, the light falling into itself and cannot be foreseen. No one knows what happens to the light when it falls into a black hole, but it has been suggested that it may fall through the black holes into another universe.

As the stars grow older the atomic power begins to burn itself out and stars go through various stages until they die. Sometimes they collide with each other and form a nova or new star.

We now know that every object in the universe has a positive and negative. There are positive and negative particles, neutrons and anti-neutrons, left and right and on earth there is good and evil as well as left and right hands.

The laws of the universe are immutable and affect everything in existence. I believe that if we, as humans, interfere with the laws of nature, nature will punish us. Evil men and women come eventually to a bad end. I do not believe in the Christian conception of hell, but evil people create their own private hell and can have adverse effects on other people.

One only needs to look at the harm caused by such evil men as Hitler and Stalin to realise the amount of harm they can inflict on other people. For most of us there is a mixture of good and evil, so the situation is to some degree flexible.

There is another factor which alarms me greatly and that is whether some of the activities of scientists are against the laws of nature. I refer particularly to splitting the atom to create atomic power. Could this discovery not be against the laws of nature? I believe that it is, and that we are in danger of destroying the world in which we live.

There may well be other discoveries which could have unforeseen results through distorting the balance of nature.

It seems likely that among the millions of stars in the universe there must be planets which have evolved in a similar way to ours and which have destroyed themselves or been destroyed.

One thing seems certain, and that is, where water exists and the atmosphere is not excessively cold, life will in time develop into some form or other. As the sun begins to die, so will the life on its planets, and there is no such thing as eternal life.

What arises out of this is pure speculation on my part. It seems to me that universal forces control the universe. Does anything control these universal forces or is everything just blind chance? It is hard for any human being to comprehend the existence of intelligence on such a vast scale as this, or of what form it could take, but this does not mean that it does not exist.

I am inclined to believe that it does exist in some form or another, but here again we are inhibited by the teaching of the religious, who always create their beliefs in relation to themselves.

Who can seriously believe in God the Father, God the Son and God the Holy Ghost or indeed in any other of the gods created by man in his image?

I believe that some intelligence exists somewhere, and that we should try to conform to the laws of nature or whatever you like to call it, but how to understand the message does not seem possible.

One thing is certain. Humans are only a temporary occupant of earth. Like the dinosaur, we will not remain in possession indefinitely. We will possibly destroy ourselves by our own follies, but there are many other events that could make the earth uninhabitable. There is the probability of an extreme ice age, or the earth becoming too hot. There is the possibility of the earth being struck by a huge asteroid. This event seems to have destroyed the dinosaurs a long time ago.

Finally, in the course of ages, an elderly and dying sun will inevitably destroy us. Apart from the immediate danger from human folly, the other dangers to the earth could be hundreds of thousands or millions of years away, so we do not have to worry much about this or take any notice of the teachings of Nostradamus.

In conclusion …

Greed

I believe that in the modern world greed causes more harm than any of the other deadly sins. Wars are usually started because someone or organisation "covets his wife or his goods or anything that he hath" (the Bible), particularly today, when people acquire huge amounts of wealth very quickly. All money has come from somewhere, either by institutions or other people.

Sooner or later governments will react and people will be charged with high rates of income tax — it would not be unreasonable to charge 80% tax for those who earn more than one million dollars a year.

Religion

The other main cause of strife in the world is religious fanaticism that has developed recently in the Islamic world. This was always the case in some form or other. In the Middle Ages the Inquisition burnt heretics alive and 'witches' were also burnt alive at the stake. Today's fanatics are as bad as their predecessors but have learnt more refined ways of effective use of their fanaticism. I refer of course to the people who blow themselves up — the suicide bombers — believing that this will entitle them to a permanent place in paradise.

Islam was the tolerant religion. Jews and other religious sects were welcome in the Islamic Empire and many Jews still live in Turkey. There is a synagogue in Istanbul.

The whole thing borders on the ridiculous. The Jews, in a pagan world, developed the doctrine of One God and the Old Testament interpreted it.

Jesus was brought up a Jew, and it is generally thought his father was the chief rabbi. He would certainly not have been permitted to cleanse the synagogue otherwise. The difference between Christianity and Judaism is mainly the grouping of the pagan belief onto Judaism by the Emperor Constantine to encourage his subjects to become Christians. There is no other justification for the persecution of Jews except the need at that time for a universal religion to back the Roman Empire.

I believe that the only way of tackling religious persecution is through enlightened education.

I am a rationalist and believe that you cannot prove that God exists but you cannot prove that he does not exist. I have an uneasy feeling that there is something in the universe beyond human comprehension, that influences exist in the universe of which we are unaware.

It is plain that left and right exist and so therefore, do good and evil. Such a complex affair as the universe must have some sort of meaning. It seems most unlikely that this meaning applies only to humans, and the probability must be that life exists elsewhere in the universe in some form.

The human race has shown the depths to which humans can fall, but also the extreme heights to which they can rise. Beethoven's works, Shakespeare, Michelangelo and the phenomenon of Jesus illustrate this. Jesus is certainly not the Son of God, I do not accept him as that, but I believe that he was something very special and I completely accept and try to follow his ethical teaching. He was probably the first socialist.

Here is a question to ponder: if you commit a sin and you are not aware that you have done so, is it in fact a sin?

The churches of the world should be trying to discover what the secrets of the universe are. Only by discovering some of these secrets can they hope to fight the forms of evil, which appear to be increasingly victorious today.

The only people who are making some progress in researching these secrets are the scientists. Let us hope they do so before other researchers destroy the world in which we live through the competitive use of the atom bomb, which will destroy us all.

With great-grandson, George.

APPENDIX

Obituary: Lady Harris

The Dominion Post, 6 March 2003

Stirrer for the persecuted

Patricia, Lady Harris: Born Cobar NSW June 14, 1910; married 1933 Jack Wolfred Ashford Harris, 1 daughter, 2 sons; educated at home and at Abbotsleigh School for Girls (Sydney) 1923–28; former actor, broadcaster, cookbooks author, founder president NZ Housewives Association, patron of Abortion Law Reform NZ, patron of the NZ Foundation for Women's Refuges; QSM (community service) 1986; died Waikanae, February 27, 2003.

Patricia Clapin Harris, 92 when she died, was a self-confessed stirrer.

An opinionated liberal, feminist, atheist, columnist, writer and wife of baronet Sir Jack Harris, she also had socialist inclinations inspired, she said, by her grandfather, a one-time president of the Methodist church in Australia.

Support the persecuted, he said, and never have anything to do with the persecutor. "That's the basis of my stirring," she said in a 1990 interview with Pauline Swain, "and of any political affiliations I have."

She took her grandfather's motivation into married life. She was a founding president of the now defunct Housewives Association, formed to protest against, among other things, food rationing in the years following World War II. Later, she became patron of the Abortion Law Reform Association and a formidable lobbyist to boot; she was one of the four joint patrons of the Women's Refuge movement, and she backed homosexual law reform.

Pat Harris was no arriviste who confided her views to the tea-and-cakes set. She willingly shared her views for causes in which she believed, and spoke eloquently in public, in broadcasts and on television.

When roused, she could be withering. She described Prime Minister Robert Muldoon as "ghastly", and when she and her husband quit the National Party and joined the Citizens For Rowling campaign in 1975, she had what she said was proof. The PM snarled at her husband and accused the Harrises of being "traitors". Nothing was further from their minds, but the distance between the PM and the Harrises became an unbridgable chasm.

A fifth generation Australian who never relinquished her citizenship, she was born Pat Penman at Cobar, the dusty and isolated mid-New South Wales copper town where her father was a mining engineer. During World War I, when her father was sent off to locate metal sources for munitions, she and her mother moved to Lake Macquarie, where she spent an idyllic childhood and was home-schooled by her mother and grandparents. When her father joined a tin mining operation in Malaya, her mother thought it was time her daughter's rough edges were smoothed at Abbotsleigh School for Girls, Sydney. The new student, who could swim like a fish, sail a boat, kept pet snakes and who had exhausted her family's library of French and English novels, found formal schooling in an academy for young ladies dreary. Her mother thwarted her plans for university studies by arranging a world tour in which the unconventional teenager would be exposed to Proper Things and, with luck, be seen as a prospective bride when the tourists swung through London. Although Miss Penman was resolutely carsick and failed to make it as a debutante, she reflected that she'd had a great deal of fun. Only on the return voyage home on the *Oronsay* in 1929 did she Meet a Man — Cambridge University history and economics graduate Jack Harris, who was New Zealand-bound. Mr Harris had been sent to New Zealand to see what he could do with a family company. Neither his father, a Liberal MP, nor an uncle were interested in living in distant New Zealand let alone involving themselves in the import and supply company their father had set up during the Otago gold rush. The neglected Bing Harris Co Ltd. was on its beam ends when Jack Harris arrived in New Zealand. He scarcely knew how to go about dealing with impending bankruptcy, let alone reconstruction. With Jack Griffin and the backing of a bank, Jack Harris rescued it in the middle of depression, expanded its manufacturing capacity, swallowed competitors and six decades later sold out to Ron Brierley.

While his commercial adventure was only beginning in 1929, Jack Harris had not forgotten his shipboard romance with Pat Penman. In the meantime, she had become, by her own account, thoroughly "bored and obnoxious" a state relieved only by her entry into professional theatre when she was selected to play the part of a Chinese girl in a J C Williamson production of the stage play *On the Spot*. Later, she was a Tahitian in the first movie version of *Mutiny on the Bounty*, starring Errol Flynn as Fletcher Christian.

"He was," she said, "quite the prettiest male creature I have ever seen in my life, except that he was absolutely gormless."

She went on to do parts in radio plays for the Australian Broadcasting Corporation and was about to become an announcer when Jack Harris visited Sydney to make his intentions plain. She would later recount how he'd not even asked if she could cook (she could, but little). They wed in 1933, and moved to her first New Zealand home — a hotel room in Dunedin.

Jack Harris had plans, however, the most important of which was to move the company's headquarters to Wellington. He'd found Dunedin stuffy. The Harrises were quickly established in Wellington, eventually setting up home in Woburn Rd, Lower Hutt, where they raised their daughter and two sons.

Pat Harris was involved in local activities. She spread the Plunket gospel and for 10 years was its Hutt president; she was founding president of the Housewives Association which campaigned for lifting rationing. Rationing of primary foodstuffs ended in 1948, but it took two more years before the state-imposed limits on remaining items were lifted.

She wrote three cookbooks, one of which, *Fit for a Sultan* (1971) was the fruit of travels in Turkey.

"The titles of their recipes are so wonderful," she exclaimed, "such as Parted Lips or Maidens' Thighs."

She wrote columns on food and reviewed books for the *NZ Listener* and *Thursday* magazine.

Jack Harris succeeded to the baronetcy held by his father, a former deputy leader of the British Liberal Party, in 1952. Pat Harris, the former Sydney broadcaster and actress, observed the title was her husband's, "not mine, but it has helped open doors". Her personal honour was a Queen's Service Medal in 1986.

The Harrises were inseparable and shared common interests, though there were differences. She did not share his interest in the Save Manapouri campaign, for example. She was an atheist, he a rationalist.

Pat and Jack Harris moved to Te Rama, a residence in the foothills above the southern banks of the Waikanae River, in 1953. In 1996 Te Rama burned down, destroying family treasures. The Harrises were devastated, and took up permanent residence at their Sydney villa. Eighteen months ago, they returned to Waikanae and moved to Parkwood village, where Sir Jack could better help manage his wife's dementia. She is survived by her husband, their daughter and two sons.

Index

A

Abortion Law Reform NZ 137
Alexandra 45
Asquith, Herbert H 16, 17, 67, 68
Auckland 8, 38, 39, 44, 79, 82

B

Baldwin, Stanley 17, 75
Barnados 58
Battersby, Sir Harry 50, 60
Becker, Count von 32
Beethoven 135
Bennett, Arnold 27
Benson, Gerald 43, 51, 52
Berlin 32-34, 68, 118
Bethnal Green 14-18, 21, 92
Bible, the 133
Big Bang 131
Bing, Mr 39
Bing Harris 14, 31, 36-58, 61-63, 77-86, 99, 138
Bledisloe, Lord 50
Bloxham family 8-10
Bond Street Models Ltd 62, 79
Bowaters 82, 83
Brandon, Phil 50
Brandt, Willi 100
Brierleys 8, 82-85, 138

C

Calder, Captain 64
Cambridge University 7, 13, 29-31, 50, 58, 118, 138
Chamberlain, Neville 67-70
Chamber of Commerce 94
Chaplin, Charlie 25
Chilco 79
China 90
Chou En-lai 90
Christian Science 21, 22
Christianity 82, 132, 134
Churchill, Sir Winston 19, 67, 69-75
Citizens For Rowling 138
Clark, Helen 98
Coates, Gordon 59, 60, 65
Cobar 56, 137, 138
cockney 25, 79
Comalco 95, 96, 99
communism 68, 69, 90, 93
communists 16, 21, 33, 34, 62, 70
Communist Party (Germany) 70
Conservative Party (UK) 15-17, 30, 67-69
Copnall, Edward Bainbridge 24
Crowley, Aleister 22
Curtin, John 73
Czechoslovakia 50, 69

D

Department of Industries & Commerce 62
Department of Trade & Industry 78
Depression, the 44, 51, 52, 59-66, 138
de la Mare, Walter 29
disease 101
Douglas, Roger 99
Dowse, Percy 92
Dunedin 7, 9, 14, 36, 38, 39, 41, 43, 44, 51-53, 57, 61, 118, 139
Dunedin Art Gallery 7, 9

E

Edward VII 15, 72
Edward VIII 74, 75
Ethel May Mantles Ltd 79
Ewen, Sir David 44
Ewen family 83, 84

F

Fleming, Charles 104
Folkes, Kenneth 63
Forbes, George W 59, 60
Ford, Henry 30
France 16, 27, 31, 32, 34, 69, 70, 121, 124
Fraser, Charles 55, 63, 77
Fraser, Peter 62, 64, 93
Fussell, Ted 60

G

Gabriel's Gully 38
General Strike (1926) 29
George V 20
George VI 20

Germany 7, 9, 31-35, 46, 50, 61, 64, 65, 67-73, 75, 77, 79, 100, 102
gold standard 30, 59
greed 133
Griffin, Jack 54, 138

H

Harris, Christopher 57, 60, 80, 85, 125, 137,139
Harris, Lady Frieda (*née* Bloxham) 9, 10, 14, 17, 19, 21-27, 29, 31, 32, 48, 53
Harris, Leslie 42, 138
Harris, Margaret 17, 57, 58, 113, 115, 125, 137,139
Harris, Lady Patricia 23, 24, 48, 54, 56-58, 60, 65, 74, 75, 80, 85, 88, 90, 92-94, 110-129, 137-39
Harris, Paul 57, 58. 125, 137,139
Harris, Sir Percy (*not* Sir Jack's father) 51
Harris, Sir Percy A 7, 8, 12-21, 26-32, 42, 46, 48, 50, 51, 53, 57, 58, 67-69, 71, 72, 74, 75, 138
Harris, Wolfred 7-11, 14, 27, 31, 37-42, 44, 46, 118
Hathaway, Joan and Brian 104-5, 107
Hitler, Adolf 22, 30, 33, 34, 65, 68-71, 75, 90, 132
Holland, Sir Sidney 92, 93
Holyoake, Sir Keith 80, 93-95
Home Guard 63
Housewives Association, NZ 92, 137,139
Hutchins, Les 97

J

Japan 63, 64, 73, 74, 77, 79, 87-89
Jesus 22, 32, 130, 134-35
Jesus Chutney 22, 32
Jewish people 7, 8, 16, 32-34, 61, 68, 69, 71, 79, 134
Johns, Bernard 66

K

Karitane Hospital 9
Kember, David 99
Keynes, John Maynard 30
Kingsford-Smith, Charles 60
Kirk, Norman 96, 98

L

Labour, first government 60
Lange, David 99, 100
Lees, W 43, 51
Liberal Democrats 58
Liberal Party 14-16, 18, 29, 58, 67, 68, 71, 74, 139
Lloyd George, David 16, 17, 67-69
London County Council 14-16, 18, 19
Lower Hutt 57, 63, 65, 93, 102, 139

M

Macky Logan's 82
Makura 49
Manapouri, Lake 95-99
Manapouri Dollar 97
Mao, Chairman 90
Marshall, Sir John 94
McLernon, Sam 77

Michelangelo 135
Milne, George 53, 55, 61, 77, 79, 83, 85, 88
Monowai, Lake 96
Muldoon, Sir Robert 90, 95, 137

N

Nash, Sir Walter 92, 93
Nathan, David 8
Nathan, Elizabeth 8, 39
Nathan, L D Ltd 8, 39
National Party 78, 93, 96, 138
Nazis 22, 33, 34, 61, 68, 69, 75
Nga Tawa School 58
Nishikawa, Mr 88, 89
Nostradamus 133
NZ Forest Products 82

O

Onehunga Woollen Mills 82
Orontes 48, 49
Otago 9, 37, 38, 45, 138
Otago University 9

P

Pankhurst, Mrs 17
pearly kings 16
Penman, Jack 107
Penman home 49
Pinker, Mr 82
Pioneer Club 8
Plunket Society 57, 92, 93, 139
Pomare, Mick 104, 118
Powell, Sir Richard 33
Presbyterian Church 14, 53
price controls 43
Prior, Dr Ian 97, 99

Q

Queen Elizabeth II Trust 107

R

Rainster 79
Ram Gopal 22
Reeves, William Pember 46
Reform Party 59
religion 8-10, 21, 53, 130, 132, 134
Reserve Bank 60
Ribbentrop, Joachim von 75
Rosen, Mr 62, 79
Ross & Glendining 44
Russia 35, 69-71, 73

S

Sargoods 44, 53, 61, 82-84
Savage, Michael 60, 62
Save Manapouri campaign 95, 97, 139
Security Intelligence Bureau 63, 64, 77
Seddon, Richard 59
Shaban 23, 24
Shakespeare 24, 27, 135
Shaw Savill & Albion 81
Simpson, Mrs 74, 75
Sinclair, Sir Archibald 18
Singapore 73
Sitwell, Edith 29
Softgoods Association 94
Stalin 70, 73, 90, 132
Strauss, Johann 33
suffragettes 17
Sutch, Dr 78, 97
Swain, Pauline 137
Sweden, Prince of 100

T

Taylor, Matthew 58
Terry, Ellen 27
Te Rama 22, 102-129, 139
Te Rauparaha 107
Thatcher, Margaret 15
Trimnell, C 43
Trinity Hall 13, 29, 50, 58
Tripp, Leonard 50
Turnbull, Mr 39
Turnbull Bing 8

U

United Party 59

V

Valentine, Graham 84, 85
Vietnam war 95
Volunteer Reserve 63

W

Waikanae 102-129, 139
Wanganui Collegiate 58
Wellington 8, 43, 47, 49-56, 59, 60, 62, 65, 77, 81, 92, 96, 139
Wellington Club 47, 50, 65, 97, 99
Wellington, Duke of 47
Williamson, JC 50, 139
Woburn 57, 93, 94, 102, 139
Women's Refuge 137
World War I 9, 16-18, 26, 42, 43, 67, 72, 87, 118, 138
World War II 16, 18, 19, 25, 26, 62, 67, 69, 76, 106, 137